MORE
OF THE
FOUR
INGREDIENT
COOKBOOK ®

By Linda Coffee and Emily Cale

D1469268

Published by Linda Coffee and Emily Cale

ACKNOWLEDGEMENTS

Many thanks to Braswell Printing for all their help and consideration! We really want to acknowledge Phil Houseal who made working on the computer look so easy!

And a special thanks to all of you who so kindly purchased our first cookbook, *The Four Ingredient Cookbook*, reordered more for friends and family, and shared your recipes with us for this cookbook!

to busy people everywhere...

We're still cooking!

With the startling success of our first cookbook, *The Four Ingredient Cookbook*, we realized that we were not alone! We were not the only ones that had hectic lives, leaving us too tired or too busy to cook. We've received hundreds of letters thanking us for writing a no-nonsense type of cookbook and asking for more.

So, thanks to the many of you that have shared your little recipes, we now have our second cookbook — *More of the Four Ingredient Cookbook*. We hope you will continue to enjoy these simple, concise and easy to follow recipes.

Thank you for all your support!

Happy "little" cooking,

Linda Coffee   Emily Cale

TABLE OF CONTENTS

APPETIZERS 7

SALADS 23

VEGETABLES 35

MAIN DISHES 51
    Beef 52
    Poultry 65
    Pork 75
    Fish 82

DESSERTS 91
    Pies 92
    Cakes 97
    Cookies 101
    Candy 105
    Other 111

STANDARD EQUIPMENT USED IN
THE FOUR INGREDIENT COOKBOOK

- ❏ Baking Sheet - 15"x10"x1"
- ❏ Basting Brush
- ❏ Blender
- ❏ Cake Pans - layer
- ❏ 5"x9" loaf, 9"x13" sheet, tube cake
- ❏ Can Opener
- ❏ Covered Casseroles
- ❏ Cookie Sheets
- ❏ Colander
- ❏ Cutting Board
- ❏ Double Boiler
- ❏ Draining Spoon
- ❏ Electric Mixer
- ❏ Grater
- ❏ Knives and Knife Sharpener
- ❏ Measuring Cups - liquid (glass) and dry
- ❏ Measuring Spoons
- ❏ Mixing Bowls - assorted
- ❏ Mixing Spoons and Wooden Spoons
- ❏ Muffin Pan
- ❏ Pie Pan - 9"
- ❏ Roasting Pan, Rack, Lid
- ❏ Rolling Pin
- ❏ Saucepans With Covers
- ❏ Skillets With Covers
- ❏ Spatula
- ❏ Vegetable Peeler
- ❏ Whisk

APPETIZERS

ARTICHOKE RANCH DIP

1. 1 Can (8 1/2 oz.) Artichoke Hearts (drained and finely chopped)
2. 1 Tablespoon Ranch Salad Dressing Mix
3. 1 Package (8 oz.) Cream Cheese (softened)
4. 1 Cup Mayonnaise

Mix above ingredients and refrigerate. Serve with crackers.

MEXICAN AVOCADO DIP

1. 3 Large Ripe Avocados (mashed)
2. 1 Cup Sour Cream
3. 1 Package Good Season Mexican Salad Dressing Mix
4. 1 Tablespoon Lemon Juice

Mix above ingredients or process in food processor until smooth. Serve with tortilla chips.

BEAN AND CHEESE DIP

1. 1 Carton (6 oz.) Garlic and Herbs Soft Spreadable Cheese
2. 1 Can Bean With Bacon Soup
3. 1 Cup Sour Cream
4. 1/2 Teaspoon Onion Powder

In saucepan, melt cheese with soup. Add sour cream and onion. Heat for 5 minutes on low heat. Serve with tortilla chips.

BLEU VEGETABLE DIP

1. 1 1/2 Cups Buttermilk
2. 2 Cups Mayonnaise
3. 1/4 Cup Crumbled Bleu Cheese
4. 1/2 Package Italian Salad Dressing Mix

Mix above ingredients and serve with assorted fresh vegetables.

CURRY DIP

1. 1 Cup Sour Cream
2. 1/2 Teaspoon Curry Powder
3. 1/4 Teaspoon Salt

Mix above ingredients and serve with fresh shrimp.

SALSA CHEESE DIP

1. 1 Cup Picante Sauce or Salsa
2. 1 Pound Velveeta Cheese (cubed)
3. 2 Tablespoons Chopped Cilantro

Melt cheese and salsa over low heat in saucepan until cheese is melted. Stir in cilantro. Serve hot with tortilla chips.

SHRIMP DIP

1. 1 Carton (8 oz.) Sour Cream
2. 1 Package (8 oz.) Cream Cheese (softened)
3. 1 Package Italian Salad Dressing Mix
4. 1 Can (4 1/4 oz.) Shrimp (drained, finely chopped))

Mix above ingredients and chill. Serve with crackers.

VEGGIE DIPPIN' DIP

1. 1 Package (8 oz) Cream Cheese (softened)
2. 2 Tablespoons Milk
3. 1 Teaspoon Prepared Horseradish
4. 1/2 Cup Parsley

Mix above ingredients and beat until smooth. Serve with raw vegetables.

ALMOND DELIGHT DIP

1. 2 Cartons (8 oz. each) Vanilla Low Fat Yogurt
2. 1/8 Teaspoon Almond Extract
3. 2 Tablespoons Chopped Toasted Almonds

Combine yogurt and almond extract. Chill at least 1 hour. Sprinkle with chopped almonds. Serve with apple slices. (To prevent apple slices from darkening, toss with lemon juice.)

BLEU CHEESE WALNUT DIP

1. 4 Ounces Cream Cheese (softened)
2. 1/4 Cup Crumbled Bleu Cheese
3. 1 Carton (12 oz.) Cottage Cheese
4. 2 Tablespoons Walnuts (finely chopped)

Blend first three ingredients until smooth. Stir in walnuts. Serve with fresh fruit.

CARAMEL FRUIT DIP

1. 1 Package (8 oz.) Cream Cheese (softened)
2. 1/2 Cup Brown Sugar
3. 1 Teaspoon Vanilla
4. 1 Cup Sour Cream

Mix above ingredients and chill. Serve with assorted fresh fruit.

PEPPERED CHEESE BALL

1. 1 Package (8 oz.) Cream Cheese (softened)
2. 1 Tablespoon Sour Cream
3. 1 Teaspoon Garlic Powder
4. 3 Tablespoons Cracked Peppercorns (retain 1 T. for garnish)

Beat first 3 ingredients. Add two tablespoons cracked peppercorns and beat until fluffy. Shape into ball. Garnish with remaining 1 tablespoon peppercorn. Refrigerate. Serve with crackers.

POTATO CHIP CHEESE APPETIZERS

1. 1/2 Cup Ranch Flavored Potato Chips (finely crushed)
2. 1 Package (8 oz.) Cream Cheese (softened)
3. 1/2 Cup Raw Carrot (grated)
4. Chopped Parsley

Mix first three ingredients and shape into tiny bite-sized balls. Roll in parsley and refrigerate until ready to serve.

DEVILED HAM LOG

1. 2 Cans (4 1/2 oz. each) Deviled Ham
2. 3 Tablespoons Pimiento Stuffed Green Olives (chopped)
3. 1 Tablespoon Prepared Mustard
4. 1 Package (8 oz.) Cream Cheese (softened)

Mix above ingredients. Form into log and chill. Serve with crackers.

SMOKED OYSTER LOAF

1. 1 Can (3 3/4 oz.) Smoked Oysters (drained, chopped)
2. 1 Package (8 oz.) Cream Cheese (softened)
3. 2 Tablespoons Worcestershire Sauce
4. 2 Tablespoons Lipton Onion Soup Mix

Mix above ingredients and shape into loaf. Refrigerate. Serve with crackers.

COCKTAIL SAUSAGE BALLS

1. 1 Pound Hot Bulk Sausage
2. 3 Cups Biscuit Mix
3. 1 Jar (8 oz.) Cheez Whiz

Mix above ingredients and shape into cocktail-sized meatballs. Place on baking pan and bake for 25 minutes or until lightly browned at 300°.

WHEAT CHEESE SNACKS

1. 1 Cup Margarine
2. 2 Cups (8 oz.) Shredded American Cheese
3. 8-10 Cups (17.2 oz. box) Spoon-size Shredded Wheat
4. 1 Tablespoon Cajun Seasoning

Melt margarine and cheese over low heat. In a large bowl, pour cheese mixture over shredded wheat and cajan seasoning. Toss to coat. Spread on cookie sheet to cool. Store in airtight container. If snacks become soft, re-crisp them by placing on baking sheet in a 250° oven for 45-60 minutes, stirring occasionally.

To keep cut fruits from discoloring, sprinkle lemon or pineapple juice over them.

MINI QUICHES

1. 1 Can Refrigerator Butterflake Biscuits
2. 1 Cup Monterey Jack With Pepper Cheese (shredded)
3. 2 Eggs
4. 2 Green Onions With Tops (finely chopped)

Separate rolls and divide each roll into three sections. Press dough section in lightly greased mini-muffin cups stretching slightly to form shell. Mix cheese, eggs and onions and spoon mixture into shells. Bake for 15 minutes or until firm at 375°.

TORTILLA ROLLUPS

1. 1 Package (8 oz.) Cream Cheese (softened)
2. 1 Teaspoon Taco Seasoning
3. 1/3 Cup Picante Sauce
4. 12 Flour Tortillas

Beat cream cheese until smooth. Add taco seasoning, picante sauce and mix well. Spread mixture on each tortilla. Roll tortilla tightly. Place seam side down in airtight container. Chill at least two hours. Slice each roll into 1-inch slices forming a pinwheel. Arrange on plate to serve.

MONTEREY CHEESE CRISPS

1. 1 Pound Monterey Jack Cheese (1/4-inch thick slices)
2. Cayenne Pepper

Cut cheese into 1/4-inch thick slices. Place slices 3 inches apart on a non-stick baking sheet...cheese will spread while baking. Sprinkle with cayenne pepper. Bake for 10 minutes or until golden brown at 400°, watch closely. Remove crisps and cool on paper towels. Stores well in airtight container.

CHEESE CHILE APPETIZER

1. 2 Packages (8 oz. each) Cream Cheese (softened)
2. 2 Large Eggs (slightly beaten)
3. 2 1/2 Cups Monterey Jack Cheese (shredded)
4. 1 Can (4 oz.) Chopped Green Chilies

Combine above ingredients and spread into lightly greased pan. Bake for 30 minutes at 325°. Cut into squares. Serve with tortilla chips.

CRAB DELIGHT

1. 2 Packages (8 oz. each) Cream Cheese (softened)
2. 1 Package (8 oz.) Imitation Crab Flakes
3. 2 Tablespoons Green Onions (finely chopped)
4. 1/2 Cup Bottled Horseradish Sauce

Beat cream cheese until smooth and blend in remaining ingredients. Spread into pie plate. Bake uncovered for 20 minutes at 375°. Serve with crackers or vegetables.

NIPPY SHRIMP

1. 1/2 Teaspoon Garlic
2. 1/2 Cup Chili Sauce
3. 30 Small Shrimp (shelled, cooked)
4. 10 Slices Bacon (cut into thirds)

Combine garlic and chili sauce. Pour over shrimp.
Cover and refrigerate several hours or overnight,
stirring occasionally. Fry bacon until partially cooked,
but still limp. Drain. Wrap each marinated shrimp in a
bacon piece. Secure with a wooden toothpick.
Broil 2-3 inches from heat until bacon is crisp.

HAM CRESCENT SNACKS

1. 1 Can Refrigerator Crescent Rolls
2. 4 Thin Slices Ham
3. 4 Teaspoons Prepared Mustard
4. 1 Cup Swiss Cheese (shredded)

Unroll dough into 4 long rectangles. Press perforations
to seal. Place ham slices on rectangles. Spread ham
with mustard and sprinkle with cheese. Starting at
longest side, roll up in jelly roll fashion. Cut into
1/2-inch slices. Place cut side down on ungreased
cookie sheet. Bake for 15-20 minutes or until lightly
browned at 375°.

DILL CROUTONS

1. 1 Package (24 oz.) Oyster Crackers
2. 3/4 Cup Vegetable Oil
3. 2 Tablespoons Dill Weed
4. 1 Package (2 oz.) Ranch Dressing Mix

Combine oil, dill weed and dressing mix until well blended. Add crackers and blend until all oil is absorbed. Store in airtight container.

SALAMI ROLLUPS

1. 1 Package (8 oz.) Cream Cheese (softened)
2. 1 Teaspoon Prepared Horseradish
3. 12 Ounces Salami (thinly sliced)

Combine cream cheese and horseradish. Spread 1 1/2 teaspoons of mixture on each salami slice. Roll up and secure with toothpicks. Makes 36 appetizers.

TORTELLINI APPETIZER

1. 1 Package (9 oz.) Meat Filled Tortellini (cooked, drained)
2. 1 Tablespoon Soy Sauce
3. 1 Tablespoon Olive Oil
4. 1 Tablespoon Sesame Seed

Combine soy sauce, oil and sesame seed. Pour over tortellini and toss to coat. Cover and refrigerate up to 24 hours. Preheat oven to 425°. Spread tortellini on foil lined baking sheet sprayed with Pam. Bake 15-18 minutes or until edges are golden.

SPICY PECANS

1. 1 Tablespoon Butter
2. 1/2-1 Teaspoon Cajun Seasoning (according to taste)
3. 1/2 Teaspoon Worcestershire Sauce
4. 1 Cup Pecan Halves

In oven proof skillet (cast iron works well) over medium heat, melt butter. Add worcestershire sauce and cajun seasoning. Add pecans and stir until well coated. Place skillet in 225° oven and bake for 45 minutes or until pecans are crisp.

ARTICHOKE APPETIZER

1. 1 Can (8 1/2 oz.) Artichoke Hearts (drained and chopped)
2. 6 Eggs
3. 1 Cup Grated Jack Cheese with Jalopenos
4. 12 Saltine Crackers (crushed)

Mix all ingredients and pour into a 9x9-inch pan. Bake for 45 minutes at 350°. Cut into squares. Serve hot or cold.

CRAB APPETIZERS

1. 1/2 Pound Velveeta Cheese
2. 1/4 Cup Margarine
3. 1 Can (6 oz.) Crab Meat
4. 1 Package Garlic Flavored Melba Toast

Melt cheese and margarine. Remove from heat. Add crab meat and mix. Spoon onto Melba Toast and broil until slightly browned.

HAM AND PIMIENTO SPREAD

1. 1 1/2 Cups Cooked Ham (finely chopped)
2. 1 Jar (4 oz.) Pimiento (drained, chopped)
3. 1/2 Cup Fresh Parsley (chopped)
4. 1/2 Cup Mayonnaise

Mix all ingredients and stir well. Chill. Serve on party rye bread or with crackers.

SMOKEY SPREAD

1. 8 Ounces Cheddar Cheese (shredded)
2. 1 Package (8 oz.) Cream Cheese (softened)
3. 4 Bacon Strips (cooked and crumbled)
4. 1 Tablespoon Worcestershire Sauce

Combine cheddar cheese and cream cheese. Mix until well blended. Add remaining ingredients. Mix well and chill. Serve with crackers.

BEER BREAD

1. 3 Cups Self-rising Flour
2. 3 Tablespoons Sugar
3. 1 Can (12 oz.) Beer

Mix above ingredients and pour into a greased loaf pan. Bake for 45 minutes or until golden brown at 350°.

TWIST STICKS

1. 1/2 Cup Sour Cream
2. 1/2 Package Savory Herb With Garlic Soup Mix
3. 1 Package (8 oz.) Refrigerator Crescent Rolls

Combine sour cream and soup mix. Spread out crescent rolls into one long piece of dough, pressing seams together. Spread mixture evenly onto dough. Cut dough into 1-inch strips and twist each strip loosely. Bake on ungreased cookie sheet for 12-15 minutes at 375°.

7-UP BISCUITS

1. 1/4 Cup 7-Up
2. 1/4 Cup Buttermilk
3. 2 Cups Biscuit Mix
4. 2 Tablespoons Butter (melted)

Mix first three ingredients and knead until smooth and elastic. Place on floured board and spread dough gently until 1-inch thick. Cut into biscuits and place on greased 9-inch baking pan. Brush tops with melted butter. Bake 20 minutes at 450°. Cool slightly before serving.

YAMMY BISCUITS

1. 2 3/4 Cups Biscuit Mix (retain 1/4 cup to flour board)
2. 1 Can (17 oz.) Yams in Syrup (mashed, do not drain)
3. 1/4 Cup Butter (melted)

Place biscuit mix in large bowl and cut yams and butter into it. Mix well. Knead on floured board until dough is not sticky. (Knead in additional biscuit mix, if necessary.) Pat out to 1/2-inch thickness and cut into biscuits. Bake 12-15 minutes at 400°.

If you're a chile pepper lover, an easy
appetizer is to cut them in half lengthwise
and fill them with tuna, chicken or egg salad
or all three.

SALADS

LIME COKE SALAD

1. 1 Package (6 oz.) Lime Jello plus 1 Cup Boiling Water
2. 1 Cup Regular Coke
3. 1 Medium Bottle (10 oz.) Maraschino Cherries (drained and chopped)
4. 1 Cup Pecans (chopped)

Dissolve jello in hot water. Add coke, cherries and pecans. Place in serving dish. Refrigerate until firm.

FRUIT COCKTAIL SALAD

1. 1 Can (17 oz.) Fruit Cocktail
2. 1 Package (3 oz.) Strawberry Jello
3. 1 Package (3 oz.) Cream Cheese (softened)
4. 1 Carton (8 oz.) Cool Whip

Heat fruit cocktail with juice and jello to boiling point. Remove from heat. Add cream cheese and stir until it melts. Fold in cool whip. Place in serving container and refrigerate.

ICE CREAM SALAD

1. 1 Package (3 oz.) Orange Jello plus 1 Cup Boiling Water
2. 1 Pint Vanilla Ice Cream (softened)
3. 1/2 Cup Pecans (chopped)
4. 1 Can (8 oz.) Crushed Pineapple (drained)

Dissolve jello in boiling water. Mix in remaining ingredients and place in serving dish. Refrigerate until set.

MANGO SALAD

1. 2 Packages (3 oz. each) Lemon Jello plus 2 Cups Boiling Water
2. 1 Jar (26 oz.) Mango With Juice (mashed)
3. 1 Package (8 oz.) Cream Cheese (softened)

Dissolve jello in boiling water. Mix mangos, juice and cream cheese together. Combine with jello mixture. Place in serving dish. Refrigerate until set.

ORANGE SALAD

1. 1 Can (8 oz.) Crushed Pineapple (drained)
2. 1 Package (3 oz.) Orange Jello
3. 1 Carton (12 oz.) Small Curd Cottage Cheese
4. 1 Carton (8 oz.) Cool Whip

Mix pineapple, orange jello, cottage cheese. Fold in Cool Whip and chill until ready to serve.

FROZEN CRANBERRY SALAD

1. 1 Can (16 oz.) Whole Cranberry Sauce
2. 1 Can (8 oz.) Crushed Pineapple (drained)
3. 1 Banana (mashed)
4. 1 Carton (12 oz.) Cool Whip

Mix above ingredients. Place in serving container and freeze.

SLICED FROZEN FRUIT SALAD

1. 1 Can (17 oz.) Chunky Mixed Fruits
2. Lettuce
3. Cool Whip or Whipped Cream

Freeze fruit cocktail in the can. Remove from freezer
and open both ends of can. Push frozen fruit cocktail
through can and cut into 4 slices. Place on a lettuce bed
and top with Cool Whip or whipped cream.

LAYERED FRUIT SALAD

1. 3 Cups Orange Sections
2. 1 Can (15 1/4 oz.) Crushed Pineapple (drained)
3. 1/2 Cup Flaked Coconut
4. 3 Tablespoons Honey

Layer 1 1/2 cups oranges, 1/2 pineapple, 1/4 cup
coconut. Repeat layer. Drizzle with honey and cover.
Chill overnight.

WALDORF SALAD

1. 4 Cups Apples (chopped)
2. 3/4 Cup Raisins
3. 1/2 Cup Pecans (pieces)
4. 1/2 Cup Mayonnaise

Combine ingredients. Refrigerate until ready to serve.

MANDARIN SALAD

1. 2 Tomatoes (peeled, sliced)
2. 2 Cans (11 oz. each) Mandarin Oranges (drained)
3. 1/2 Cup Onion (thinly sliced)
4. 3 Cups Lettuce Leaves (torn into bite-size pieces)

Combine ingredients. Good served with Orange Juice Dressing. (Recipe follows.)

ORANGE JUICE DRESSING

1. 1/4 Cup Orange Juice
2. 2 Teaspoons Red Wine Vinegar .
3. 1 Tablespoon Vegetable Oil
4. 2 Teaspoons Honey

Mix above ingredients and pour over mandarin salad.

FROZEN PINEAPPLE CRANBERRY SALAD

1. 1 Can (20 oz.) Crushed Pineapple (drained)
2. 1 Can (16 oz.) Whole Cranberry Sauce
3. 1 Cup Sour Cream
4. 1/2 Cup Pecans (chopped)

Combine all ingredients and place in a 8x8-inch pan. Freeze. Cut into squares before serving.

AVOCADO GRAPEFRUIT SALAD

1. 1 Jar (26 oz.) Grapefruit Sections (drained)
2. 2 Ripe Avocados (peeled, sliced)
3. 1/2 Cup Red Onion (thinly sliced)
4. Prepared Poppy Seed Dressing

Combine grapefruit, avocados and onions. Serve with dressing on a bed of lettuce.

NUTTY BANANA SALAD

1. 2/3 Cup Mayonnaise
2. 2 Tablespoons Sugar
3. 6 Medium Bananas
4. 1 1/3 Cup Peanuts (finely chopped)

Add sugar to mayonnaise and mix well. Roll the bananas in mayonnaise mixture. Roll the bananas in the nuts. Slice and serve on a crisp bed of lettuce.

COLE SLAW

1. 1 Head Cabbage (shredded)
2. 1 Jar (4 oz.) Pimiento (chopped)
3. 1 Can (12 oz.) Peanuts
4. 1 Cup Mayonnaise

Blend mayonnaise with the fluid from the pimientos. Combine all ingredients and chill.

MARINATED ASPARAGUS SALAD

1. 1 Can (15 oz.) Asparagus Pieces (drained)
2. 1 Can (8 1/2 oz.) Small Early Peas (drained)
3. 3 Hard Boiled Eggs (chopped)
4. 1 Package Garlic Salad Dressing Mix (prepared)

Combine asparagus, peas and eggs. Pour dressing over mixture and stir gently. Cover and chill several hours. Drain and serve on a lettuce bed.

CORN SALAD

1. 2 Cans (16 oz. each) Mexicorn (drained)
2. 1 Green Pepper (chopped)
3. 1 Onion (chopped)
4. 1 Cup Catalina Salad Dressing

Combine ingredients. Chill several hours. Serve cold.

CUCUMBER SALAD

1. 4 Large Cucumbers (peeled and sliced)
2. 2 Onions (sliced)
3. 1/2 Teaspoon Sugar
4. 1 Cup Sour Cream

Place cucumbers and onions in bowl. Sprinkle with sugar. Add sour cream and mix. Salt and pepper to taste. Refrigerate for several hours.

PEA SALAD

1. 1 Package (10 oz.) Frozen Green Peas (thawed)
2. 1/2 Cup Chedder Cheese (cubed)
3. 1/2 Cup Celery (chopped)
4. 1/2 Cup Sour Cream

Combine above ingredients. Salt and pepper to taste.
Refrigerate for several hours. Serve on bed of lettuce.

SPINACH SALAD

1. 1 Pound Spinach (torn into bite-size pieces)
2. 1 Medium Red Onion (thinly sliced)
3. 1 Can (11 oz.) Mandarin Oranges (drained)
4. 1/2 Cup Almonds (toasted)

Combine ingredients. Good served with poppy seed
dressing.

SUNNY SPINACH SALAD

1. 1 Pound Spinach (torn into bite-size pieces)
2. 1 Medium Red Onion (thinly sliced)
3. 1 Package (6 oz.) Dried Apricots (chopped)
4. 1/3 Cup Toasted Salted Sunflower Seeds

Combine ingredients. Good served with vinaigrette
dressing.

SUPER SPINACH SALAD

1. 1 Pound Spinach (torn into bite-size pieces)
2. 8 Ounces Fresh Mushrooms (sliced)
3. 8 Slices Bacon (fried and crumbled)

Place spinach, mushrooms and crumbled bacon in salad bowl. Serve with Italian or Ranch salad dressing.

GREEN BEAN SALAD

1. 1 Can (16 oz.) French Style Green Beans (drained)
2. 8 Cherry Tomatoes (halved)
3. 4 Fresh Green Onions (sliced)
4. 1/2 Cup French Dressing

Combine ingredients. Chill at least one hour before serving. Serve on a crisp bed of lettuce.

CARROT SALAD

1. 2 Cups grated Carrots
2. 1/2 Cup Raisins
3. 1 Can (8 3/4 oz.) Pineapple Tidbits (drained)
4. 1/3 Cup Mayonnaise

Combine above ingredients and serve on a crisp bed of lettuce.

RICE SALAD

1. 1/2 Cup Italian Salad Dressing
2. 1/2 Cup Mayonnaise
3. 1 Package (10 oz.) Frozen Mixed Vegetables (thawed)
4. 3 Cups Cooked Rice

Blend Italian dressing and mayonnaise. Stir in vegetables and rice. Toss well. Chill until ready to serve.

SEAFOOD SALAD

1. 1 Package (8 oz.) Crab Delights (flake style)
2. 1/2 Cup Mayonnaise
3. 2 Stalks Celery (chopped)
4. 3 Tablespoons Onion (finely chopped)

Combine ingredients. Serve on a crisp bed of lettuce.

SHRIMP AND RICE SALAD

1. 2 Cups Cooked Rice
2. 12 Ounces Shrimp (peeled, cooked)
3. 1 Package (10 oz.) Frozen Peas/Pearl Onions (thawed)
4. 1/2 Cup Italian Salad Dressing

Mix above ingredients and serve on a crisp bed of lettuce.

PASTA SALAD

1. 1 Package (16 oz.) Elbow Macaroni Pasta (cooked, rinsed, drained)
2. 1 Medium Sweet Red Pepper (cut into strips)
3. 1 Cup Fresh Mushrooms (sliced)
4. 1 Cup Broccoli Flowerets

Combine ingredients and toss well. Chill and serve with Caesar salad dressing.

SEAFOOD PASTA SALAD

1. 1 Pound Vegetable Rotini Pasta (cooked, rinsed, drained)
2. 1 Can (6 oz.) Pitted Ripe Olives
3. 1 Package (10 oz.) Frozen Chopped Broccoli (thawed, drained)
4. 1 Package (8 oz.) Imitation Crab Flakes

Combine pasta with remaining ingredients. Toss and chill until ready to serve. Serve with Italian or Ranch salad dressing.

Never put tomatoes in the refrigerator, the cold temperature stops the ripening process and kills tomato flavor.

VEGETABLES

MARINATED ARTICHOKE HEARTS

1. 2 Packages (9 oz. each) Frozen Artichoke Hearts
2. 1 Kraft House Italian With Olive Oil Salad Dressing

Cook artichoke hearts as directed on package. Drain well. Cool. Pour salad dressing over artichokes. Toss and refrigerate overnight.

LEMON ASPARAGUS AND BABY CARROTS

1. 1 Pound Asparagus (steamed until crisp tender)
2. 1/2 Pound Small Carrots (steamed until crisp tender)
3. Lemon Pepper
4. 1 Tablespoon Lemon Juice

Drain asparagus and carrots. In casserole, combine carrots and asparagus. Cover and refrigerate. When ready to serve, sprinkle with lemon pepper and lemon juice. Serve cold.

ASPARAGUS IN LEMON BUTTER

1. 1 Pound Asparagus (remove tough stems)
2. 2 Tablespoons Butter (melted)
3. 1/2 Teaspoon Grated Lemon Peel
4. 2 Tablespoons Fresh Lemon Juice

Cut asparagus in pieces about 1 1/2-inches long. Simmer asparagus in water, enough to cover, for about 6 minutes or until crisp-tender. Drain. In saucepan combine all ingredients. Cook over medium heat for 2 minutes. Stir and serve warm.

ASPARAGUS WITH CURRY SAUCE

1. 2 Packages (10 oz. each) Frozen Asparagus Spears
2. 1/2 Cup Mayonnaise
3. 2 Teaspoons Curry Powder
4. 1 1/2 Teaspoon Lemon Juice

Cook asparagus and drain. Combine mayonnaise, curry powder and lemon juice. Pour over asparagus. Serve warm.

SAUTEED BROCCOLI

1. 1 Package (10 oz.) Frozen Broccoli
2. 1 Package (10 oz.) Frozen Whole Kernel Corn
3. 1 Can (4 oz.) Sliced Mushrooms (drained)
4. 1/2 Cup Margarine

Melt margarine in large skillet. Saute broccoli, corn and mushrooms in melted margarine until crisp-tender. Serve warm. Season to taste.

ITALIAN STYLE BROCCOLI

1. 1 1/2 Pounds Broccoli (cut into flowerets)
2. 1/4 Cup Olive Oil
3. 2 Cloves Garlic (minced)
4. 2 Tablespoons Lemon Juice

Steam broccoli in large skillet for 5 minutes until crispy tender. Remove broccoli and drain. Pour oil into skillet and add garlic. Cook over medium heat stirring constantly until garlic is lightly browned. Add broccoli and lemon juice. Toss gently. Cover and cook for an additional minute.

BRUSSELS SPROUTS

1. 2 Packages (10 oz. each) Frozen Brussels Sprouts (cooked, drained)
2. 4 Tablespoons Margarine
3. 1/3 Cup Soft Bread Crumbs
4. 4 Teaspoons Lemon Juice

In a small skillet, saute bread crumbs and 1 tablespoon margarine. Remove bread crumbs. Add remaining 3 tablespoons margarine and lemon juice to skillet. Stir until margarine is melted. Add sprouts, toss until evenly coated and thoroughly heated. Place in serving dish. Sprinkle with bread crumbs and serve.

DILL CARROTS

1. 1 Pound Carrots (peeled and sliced)
2. 1/2 Cup Italian Dressing
3. 1/2 Cup Green Goddess Dressing
4. 1 Tablespoon Dillweed

Cook carrots until crispy tender and drain. Mix Italian Dressing, Green Goddess Dressing and dillweed together. Pour dressing mixture over carrots. Refrigerate overnight. Serve cold.

To restore sweetness in old vegetables, add
a little sugar to water while cooking.

CHEESY CAULIFLOWER

1. 1 Bag (16 oz.) Frozen Cauliflower (cooked, drained)
2. 1 Can Cream of Chicken Soup
3. 1/4 Cup Milk
4. 1 Cup Swiss Cheese (shredded)

Place cauliflower in baking dish. Combine soup, milk and cheese and spread over cauliflower. Bake for 10 minutes at 350°.

SCALLOPED CORN

1. 2 Eggs (slightly beaten)
2. 1 Cup Milk
3. 1 Cup Cracker Crumbs
4. 2 Cans (16 oz. each) Whole Corn (drained)

Blend all ingredients together. Bake in lightly greased loaf pan for 1 hour at 325°.

CORN RELISH

1. 2 Cans (11 oz. each) Mexican-style Corn
2. 1/3 Cup Sugar
3. 1/3 Cup Cider Vinegar
4. 1/3 Cup Sweet Pickle Relish

Combine above ingredients and bring to a boil. Simmer for 5 minutes. Remove from heat, cover and refrigerate.

FETTUCINE ALFREDO

1. 1 Package (8 oz.) Fettucine (cooked, drained)
2. 6 Tablespoons Margarine
3. 1/2 Cup Grated Parmesan Cheese
4. 2 Tablespoons Half and Half

In saucepan over low heat, melt margarine. Add half and half and cheese. Heat thoroughly and pour over fettucine and toss. Serve warm.

GREEN BEAN CASSEROLE

1. 2 Cans (16 oz. each) Whole Green Beans (drained)
2. 1/2 Cup French Dressing
3. 1/2 Cup Onion (chopped)
4. 6-9 Strips Bacon (cooked, crumbled)

Combine first 3 ingredients. Place in casserole. Sprinkle with bacon and bake for 30 minutes at 350°.

GREEN CHILE CASSEROLE

1. 1 Can (4 oz.) Green Chilies (chopped)
2. 1 Can Cream of Chicken Soup
3. 1 Package (8 oz.) Colby Cheese (grated)
4. 10-12 Corn Tortillas (cut into wedges)

Mix soup with green chilies. Layer tortillas and cheese. Pour soup mixture over top and sprinkle with remaining cheese. Bake for 30 minutes at 350°.

MARVELOUS MUSHROOMS

1. 1 Pound Fresh Mushrooms (remove stems)
2. 2 Tablespoons Vegetable Oil
3. 2 1/2 Tablespoons Chopped Garlic
4. 2 Tablespoons Soy Sauce

Cut mushroom stems off. Heat oil in frying pan and add garlic. Cook garlic over medium-low heat around 4-6 minutes. Do not let garlic burn. Add mushrooms and cook 2-3 minutes. Add soy sauce; toss and serve immediately.

STIR FRIED MUSHROOMS WITH BACON

1. 4 Slices Bacon (cut 1/2-inch pieces)
2. 8 Ounces Fresh Mushrooms (sliced)
3. 1/4 Cup Cooking Sherry

Stir fry bacon until crisp. Remove bacon, reserving drippings. Add mushrooms and stir fry for 5-10 minutes. Drain off excess fat. Add wine and bacon and simmer for 3 minutes.

POPPY SEED NOODLES

1. 1 Package (8 oz.) Wide Noodles (cooked, drained)
2. 1/4 Cup Butter (melted)
3. 2 Tablespoons Poppy Seeds

Toss noodles with butter and poppy seeds. Season to taste.

OKRA SUCCOTASH

1. 3 Cups Okra (sliced)
2. 1 Can (16 oz.) Corn
3. 1 Can (14 1/2 oz.) Seasoned Stewed Tomatoes
4. 1/2 Cup Onion (chopped)

Rinse okra under running water. Drain. Combine ingredients in a large skillet. Cover and simmer for 15 minutes. Season to taste.

SPICY POTATOES

1. 4 Large Baking Potatoes
2. 1/4 Cup Olive Oil
3. 1 Package Onion Soup Mix

Cut potatoes into bite-sized chunks. Toss potatoes in oil and onion soup mix to coat. Place on baking sheet. Bake for 45 minutes at 375°.

PARSLEY NEW POTATOES

1. 2 Cans (16 oz. each) Sliced New Potatoes (drained)
2. 1/4 Cup Margarine (melted)
3. 6 Tablespoons Fresh Parsley (chopped)

Place new potatoes in buttered casserole. Mix margarine and parsley and pour over potatoes. Bake 20 minutes at 350°. Season to taste.

ITALIAN POTATOES

1. 4 Medium Potatoes (cut in half lengthwise)
2. 1/4 Cup Butter
3. 1 Envelope Italian Salad Dressing Mix
4. 1/3 Cup Grated Parmesan Cheese

Spread butter on potato halves. Sprinkle salad dressing and cheese over potatoes. Bake on greased baking sheet, cut-size down, for 45 minutes at 400°.

QUICK POTATO CHEESE BAKE

1. 4 Cups Mashed Potatoes
2. 1/2 Cup Parmesan Cheese
3. 2 Eggs (slightly beaten)
4. 1/2 Cup Cheddar Cheese (grated)

Combine potatoes, parmesan cheese and eggs. Season to taste. Place in casserole. Top with cheddar cheese and bake for 25 minutes at 350°.

SCALLOPED POTATOES

1. 8 Large Potatoes (thinly sliced)
2. 1 Can Cream of Chicken Soup
3. 1 Can Cheddar Cheese Soup
4. 1 Can Milk

Slice potatoes in 1/4-inch slices. Mix soups and milk. Layer potatoes and soup mix. Top with soup mix. Bake 45 minutes or until potatoes are tender at 350°.

COUNTRY STYLE POTATOES

1. 2 Cans (16 oz. each) New Potatoes (drained, sliced)
2. 2 Tablespoons Margarine (melted)
3. 1 Teaspoon Basil
4. 1 Medium Onion (chopped)

Melt margarine in skillet. Add potatoes and basil.
Cook until potatoes are lightly browned, stirring
occasionally. Add chopped onion and cook a few
minutes longer. (Onion should be hot, but still crisp.)

POTATOES AU GRATIN

1. 1 Cup Half and Half
2. 1 Package (32 oz.) Hash Brown Potatoes (thawed)
3. 2 Tablespoons Margarine
4. 1/2 Cup Cheddar Cheese (grated)

Heat half and half in sauce pan. Add potatoes and
margarine. Simmer slowly until thickened. Pour into
lightly greased baking dish. Sprinkle with cheese.
Place under broiler. Broil until brown.

CHICKEN FLAVORED WHIPPED POTATOES

1. 1 Cup Instant Mashed Potatoes Flakes
2. 3 Cups Hot Water
3. 1 Tablespoon Chicken Bouillon Granules
4. 1 Tablespoon Margarine

Dissolve chicken bouillon and margarine in hot water.
Add to potatoes and mix well. Season to taste.

NEW POTATOES VINAIGRETTE

1. 2 Cans (16 oz. each) New Potatoes
2. 1/4 Cup Vinaigrette Dressing
3. 1 Tablespoon Fresh Parsley (chopped)

Heat potatoes thoroughly. Drain. Place in bowl and toss gently with dressing. Sprinkle with parsley and serve.

STUFFED BAKED SWEET POTATOES

1. 6 Medium Sweet Potatoes
2. 2 Tablespoons Margarine
3. 1 Can (8 oz.) Crushed Pineapple (drained)
4. 1/2 Cup Pecans (chopped)

Bake potatoes for 1 hour at 375°. Cut a 1-inch lengthwise wedge from the top of each potato. Carefully scoop pulp from shells. Mix potato pulp, margarine and pineapple. Beat until fluffy. Stuff back into potato shell and sprinkle with pecans. Bake for 12 minutes at 375°.

To keep spaghetti and macaroni from sticking, add 1 tablespoon olive oil for flavor.

MARSHMALLOW TOPPED SWEET POTATOES

1. 1 Can (17 oz.) Yams (drained, cut in half)
2. 2 Tablespoons Margarine
3. 1/3 Cup Honey
4. 1/2 Cup Miniature Marshmallows

Arrange potatoes in single layer in buttered baking pan.
Dot with margarine and drizzle with honey. Bake
20 minutes at 350°. Remove from oven and spoon
honey sauce from bottom of pan over potatoes.
Sprinkle with marshmallows and return to oven long
enough to lightly brown marshmallow topping.

FRENCH ONION RICE

1. 1 Cup Long Grain White Rice
2. 1/4 Cup Margarine
3. 1 Can Onion Soup plus 1 Can Water
4. 1 Can (4 oz.) Chopped Mushrooms

Lightly brown rice in margarine. Add soup, water and
mushrooms. Cover and simmer about 25 minutes or
until liquid is gone. Fluff and serve.

ONIONS AND HERB RICE

1. 1 Envelope Onion Soup Mix plus 2 cups water
2. 2 Tablespoons Parsley
3 1 1/2 Teaspoons Basil
4. 2 Cups Minute Rice

Combine first 3 ingredients with water and bring to a
boil. Add rice, cover and remove from heat. Let stand
for 5-10 minutes. Fluff and serve.

CUMIN RICE

1. 3 Can Chicken Broth
2. 2 Teaspoons Cumin
3. 1 1/2 Cups Uncooked Long Grain Rice
4. 1/2 Cup Green Onions (chopped)

Bring broth to a boil and add cumin and rice. Cover, reduce heat and simmer for 20 minutes or until liquid is gone. Add green onions and toss.

DIRTY RICE

1. 1 Cup Uncooked White Rice
2. 1 Stick Margarine (melted)
3. 1 Can Onion Soup
4. 1 Can Beef Bouillon

Mix all ingredients together. Cover and bake for 1 hour at 350°.

SAUTEED SPINACH

1. 1 Pound Fresh Spinach
2. 2 Tablespoons Olive Oil
3. 2 Tablespoons White Wine or Cooking Sherry
4. 1/4 Cup Freshly Grated Parmesan Cheese

Wash and dry spinach. Cook spinach in olive oil in large skillet over high heat. Stir constantly until wilted. Add wine and cook until liquid is gone. Sprinkle with parmesan cheese and serve.

SQUASH DRESSING

1. 6-8 Squash (sliced, cooked, drained)
2. 2 Cups Crumbled Mexican Corn Bread (prepared)
3. 1 Large Onion (chopped)
4. 1 Can Nacho Cheese Soup

Combine ingredients. Pour into baking pan. Bake 35-40 minutes at 350°.

POTATO CHIP SQUASH CASSEROLE

1. 4-6 Squash (partially cooked, sliced)
2. 1 Can Cream of Mushroom Soup
3. 1 Cup Crushed Ranch Flavored Potato Chips
4. 1 Cup American Cheese (grated)

In greased casserole, layer squash, soup (undiluted) and crushed potato chips. Repeat layer and top with grated cheese. Bake for 30 minutes at 350° or until bubbly.

BAKED SQUASH CASSEROLE

1. 6-8 Medium Yellow Squash (grated)
2. 1 Large Onion (grated)
3. 2 Tablespoons Melted Margarine
4. 1 Cup Bread Crumbs

Mix above ingredients. Season to taste. Pour into greased baking dish. Bake for 30-45 minutes or until brown at 350°.

FRIED GREEN TOMATOES

1. 6 Large Firm Green Tomatoes (cut 1/4-inch slices)
2. 1 Cup Cornmeal
3. Vegetable Oil
4. Salt/Pepper

Dredge tomatoes in cornmeal. Season with salt and pepper. Heat oil. Add tomatoes and fry over medium-high heat until browned. Turn once.

STIR FRY ZUCCHINI

1. 4 Cups Zucchini (sliced)
2. 1/4 Cup Margarine
3. 2 Tablespoons Lemon Pepper
4. Juice of One Lemon

Saute zucchini and lemon pepper in margarine. Cook 10-15 minutes, stirring frequently. Add lemon juice. Stir and serve.

ZUCCHINI AND WALNUTS

1. 3 Tablespoons Margarine
2. 1/2 Cup Walnuts (coarsely chopped)
3. 4 Cups Zucchini (cut into 1/2-inch slices)

Heat 1 tablespoon margarine in skillet. Add walnuts and stir until lightly brown. Remove walnuts from skillet. Heat remaining 2 tablespoons margarine and zucchini. Saute zucchini until it begins to soften. Combine walnuts with zucchini. Season to taste.

MAIN
DISHES

ZIPPY BEEF CASSEROLE Bake 350° 45 Minutes

1. 1 Box (6.8 oz.) Rice-a-Roni
2. 1 Can Nacho Cheese Soup plus 1 Can Water
3. 2 Eggs
4. 1 Pound Ground Beef (browned, drained)

Combine ingredients. Place in casserole. Cover and bake for 30 minutes at 350°, uncover and continue baking 10-15 minutes.

CONEY ISLAND BURGERS   Stove Top

1. 1 Pound Lean Ground Beef
2. 1/2 Cup Bottled BBQ Sauce
3. 4 Tablespoons Pickle Relish
4. 4 Tablespoons Onion (chopped)

Combine ingredients and form into shape of hot dogs. Saute, turning until brown and cooked through. Place in hot dog buns and serve with mustard.

MEAT PITA POCKETS   Stove top

1. 1 1/2 Pounds Ground Beef (browned, drained)
2. 1 Can Chicken Gumbo Soup (undiluted)
3. 1/3 Cup Chili Sauce
4. 6 Pita Pockets

Mix first three ingredients together and simmer for 5 to 10 minutes. Spoon filling into pita pockets. Serve.

MEXICAN MEATLOAF   Bake 350° 1 1/2 Hours

1. 2 Pounds Lean Ground Beef
2. 1 Cup Picante Sauce (2/3 cup in loaf and 1/3 cup over top of loaf)
3. 1 Cup Bread Crumbs
4. 2 Eggs (slightly beaten)

Combine above ingredients, saving 1/3 cup picante sauce for top of meatloaf. Form into a loaf and place in greased ovenproof pan. Top with the remaining sauce. Bake at 350° for 1 1/2 hours.

CHILI MEAT LOAF   Bake 350° 1 1/2 Hours

1. 2 Pounds Lean Ground Beef
2. 1 Can (15 oz.) Chili With Beans
3. 2 Eggs (slightly beaten)
4. 1 Medium Onion (chopped)

Combine ingredients. Shape into loaf and place into a greased shallow baking dish. Bake at 350° for 1 1/2 hours.

FRITO MEAT BALLS   Stove Top

1. 2 Pounds Lean Ground Beef
2. 1 Cup Fritos (crushed)
3. 1 Egg (slightly beaten)
4. 1 Can Cream of Mushroom Soup plus 1/2 Can Water

Mix meat, fritos and egg together. Form into meat balls and brown in skillet. Mix soup and water and pour over meatballs. Simmer for 30 minutes over low heat.

QUICK MEAT BALLS   Bake 350° 30 Minutes

1. 2 Pounds Lean Ground Meat
2. 1/2 Pound Sausage
3. 1 Box (6 oz.) Stove Top Dressing
4. 3 Eggs

Mix above ingredients and shape into balls. Place on baking sheet. Bake at 350° for 30 minutes.

SOUR CREAM MEATBALLS   Stove Top
                          Bake 350°   30 Minutes

1. 1 1/2 Pounds Lean Ground Beef
2. 1 Carton (8 oz.) Sour Cream
3. 1 Teaspoon Garlic Powder
4. 1 Teaspoon Salt

Mix ground beef, garlic powder, salt and 1/2 of the sour cream together. Form into balls. Brown balls in skillet and place in baking dish. Spread remaining sour cream on meatballs and bake at 350° for 30 minutes.

SPANISH HAMBURGERS   Stove Top

1. 1 Pound Lean Ground Beef
2. 1 Large Onion (chopped)
3. 1 Can Tomato Soup
4. 1 Teaspoon Chili Powder

Brown hamburger and onion. Drain off fat. Add soup and chili powder to hamburger mixture. Stir and simmer until hot. Serve over hamburger buns.

SPANISH STUFFED PEPPERS   Stove Top
Bake 350°   25 Minutes

1. 3 Green Peppers
2. 1 Pound Lean Ground Beef (browned, drained)
3. 1 Can (15 oz.) Spanish Rice
4. 2 Tablespoons Catsup

Cut green peppers in half and remove pulp from center.
Steam peppers in 1-inch of water for 5 minutes. Cool.
Brown ground beef. Drain off excess fat. Stir in
spanish rice and catsup. Spoon ingredients into green
pepper halves. Place in baking pan and bake at 350°
for 25 minutes.

CABBAGE AND BEEF DISH
Bake 350°   1 Hour

1. 1 Pound Lean Ground Beef
2. 1 Medium Onion (chopped)
3. 3 Cups Cabbage (shredded)
4. 1 Can Tomato Soup

Brown ground beef and onion. Drain and season to
taste. Spread in baking dish. Top with 3 cups cabbage.
Pour tomato soup on top and cover. Bake at 350° for
1 hour.

Casseroles are good time savers, as you can
combine all the ingredients in one casserole
and bake. Or, make two casseroles, one for
now and the other for another day.
Most casseroles freeze very well
and can be frozen right in the container in
which you cook it in.

BEEF AND CABBAGE ROLLS   Stove Top
Bake 350°10-12 Minutes

1. 1 Pound Lean Ground Beef
2. 1 Medium Onion (chopped)
3. 1 Cup Sauerkraut (drained)
4. 3 Packages Refrigerator Crescent Rolls

In a large skillet, brown beef and onions. Drain off any
excess liquid. Season to taste. Add sauerkraut and
cook until heated. Open cresent rolls and crimp
2 triangles together to form rectangles. Place small
amount of meat mixture on each rectangle. Roll up.
Slice each roll into 2 or 3 rounds. Place on greased
baking sheet, cut side down. Bake at 350° for
10 minutes or until browned.

MEAT AND POTATO DINNER   Bake 350°
45 Minutes

1. 4 Large Potatoes (peeled and sliced)
2. 1 Pound Lean Ground Beef (browned and drained)
3. Green Peppers (sliced)
4. 1 Can (28 oz.) Tomatoes (chopped)

Layer above ingredients in order given. Bake at 350°
for 45 minutes.

HOT MEAT DISH   Bake 350°   1 Hour

1. 1 1/2 Pounds Lean Ground Beef
2. 1 Package (6 oz.) Seasoned Croutons
3. 2 Cans Cream of Chicken Soup
4. 1 Soup Can of Milk

Pat ground beef into bottom of greased 9x12 casserole.
Mix croutons, soup and milk. Pour over meat and bake
at 350° for 1 hour.

VEGETABLE MEAT DISH   Bake 375   1 Hour

1. 1 Pound Lean Ground Beef (browned, drained)
2. 1 Onion (chopped)
3. 4 Large Potatoes (peeled, sliced)
4. 1 Can (10 1/2 oz.) Vegetable Beef Soup

Brown ground beef and onions; drain. Place potato
slices in lightly greased casserole. Spread ground beef
and onions over potatoes. Pour soup over top. Cover
and bake at 375° for 45 minutes. Remove cover and
continue baking 15 minutes.

GROUND BEEF AND PEPPER SKILLET   Stove Top

1. 1 Pound Lean Ground Beef
2. 1 Small Onion (chopped)
3. 1 Green Pepper (chopped)
4. 1 Jar (12 oz.) Mushroom Gravy

Brown ground beef, onion and green pepper. Drain.
Add gravy and simmer for 20-30 minutes. Serve over
rice or noodles.

FIESTA DINNER   Bake 350° 30 Minutes

1. 1 Pound Package Taco Flavored Ground Beef
   (browned, drained)
2. 1 Can (16 oz.) Tomatoes (drained, chopped)
3. 8 Ounces Colby Cheese (grated)
4. 6 Flour Tortillas

Add tomatoes to taco meat. Simmer for 15 minutes.
Layer one flour tortilla in round casserole. Place taco
meat on tortilla and spread to cover. Sprinkle with
cheese. Repeat layer starting with tortilla and ending
with cheese. Bake at 350° for 30 minutes.

RANCH STYLE SPAGHETTI Bake 325°   45 Minutes

1. 1 Pound Lean Ground Beef (browned, drained)
2. 1 Can (14 3/4 oz.) Spaghetti in Tomato Sauce
3. 1 Can (15 oz.) Ranch Style Beans
4. 8 Ounces Cheddar Cheese (grated)

Add spaghetti sauce and beans to browned meat. Place
in casserole. Top with grated cheese. Bake at 325° for
45 minutes.

HAMBURGER SLOPPY JOES   Stove Top

1. 1 Pound Lean Ground Beef
2. 1/4 Cup Catsup
3. 1 Tablespoon Mustard
4. 1 Can Chicken Gumbo Soup

Brown ground beef in skillet and drain. Combine
ingredients. Simmer for 30 minutes. Serve between
hamburger buns.

BEEF ROAST

Bake 500°15-24 Minutes
2 Hours With Oven Off

1. 3-4 Pound Eye of Round Roast
2. Cracked Peppercorns

Preheat oven to 500°. Roll roast in peppercorns. Place in baking dish, then in preheated oven. Bake 5-6 minutes per pound. Turn oven off and leave roast in oven for 2 more hours. DO NOT OPEN OVEN DURING THIS TIME. Bake uncovered for medium done roast. Use juice to make gravy.

MUSTARD ONION CHUCK ROAST

Bake 325°
3 Hours

1. 2 Tablespoons Dry Mustard
2. 1 1/2 Teaspoons Water
3. 3 Pounds Beef Chuck Pot Roast
4. 1/2 Cup Soy Sauce

Blend mustard with water to make a paste. Cover and let stand for 5 minutes. Place tin foil in shallow baking pan. Place meat on foil. Stir soy sauce into mustard mixture, blending until smooth. Pour mixture evenly over roast. Fold and seal foil to cover roast. Bake at 325° for 3 hours.

COKE ROAST
Bake 350°
30 Minutes Per Pound

1. Beef Brisket or Roast
2. 1 Package Dry Onion Soup Mix
3. 1 Jar (12 oz.) Chili Sauce
4. 1 Can (12 oz.) Regular Coke

Mix soup, chili sauce and coke together. Pour over roast, cover and bake at 350° for 30 minutes per pound. DO NOT USE FOIL WITH THIS BECAUSE OF COKE.

BEEF BRISKET
Bake 350°   3 Hours

1. 4-5 Pounds Beef Brisket
2. 1/4 Teaspoon Garlic Salt
3. 2 Medium Onions (sliced)
4. 3 Garlic Cloves

Place brisket in roasting pan. Season with garlic salt. Place sliced onions and garlic cloves over top of roast. Bake covered at 350° for 3 hours.

EASY POT ROAST   Stove Top

1. 3-4 Pounds Boneless Beef Pot Roast
2. 1/4 Cup Oil
3. 1 Can Golden Mushroom Soup
4. 2 Tablespoons Flour Paste (2 T. flour blended with 1/4 cup cold water)

In heavy skillet, brown meat on all sides in oil. Stir in soup and cover. Cook over low heat 3 hours, stirring occasionally. Remove meat from skillet. To thicken pan gravy, add flour paste and stir until smooth. Cook until thickened. Return meat to gravy until ready to serve.

OVEN POT ROAST AND GRAVY   Bake 350°
45 Minutes Per Pound

1. 4-5 Pounds Pot Roast
2. 1 Package Dry Onion Soup Mix
3. 1 Can Mushroom Soup

Place roast in large heavy aluminum foil in baking pan. Shake package of onion soup mix on top of pot roast. Cover roast with mushroom soup. Close foil so steam does not escape, leave an air pocket above meat. Cook at 350° about 45 minutes per pound.

SIZZLER SIRLOIN STEAK   Grill or Broil

1. 3/4 Cup Catsup
2. 1/2 Cup Worcestershire Sauce
3. 1/3 Cup Oil
4. 3 Pounds Boneless Beef Sirloin Steak

Mix catsup, worcestershire sauce and oil together. Pour over steak and marinate overnight. Remove steak from marinade and grill on outdoor grill or broil in oven about 12 minutes on each side. Brush with marinade as it is cooking.

BBQ FLANK STEAK   Broil
8 Minutes Per Side

1. 1 Package (32 oz.) Frozen French Fries
2. 1 Package (16 oz.) Frozen Onion Rings
3. 1 Bottle (1 lb. 2 oz.) Hickory Smoke BBQ Sauce
4. 2 Pounds Tenderized Flank Steak

In shallow roasting pan (2-3 inches deep), mix potatoes and onion rings. Broil for 10 minutes. Remove from oven and stir and turn potatoes and onion rings. Drizzle with half the BBQ sauce. Top with flank steak. Cover any potatoes and onion rings that are not covered by the flank steak with foil. Return to oven and broil for 8 minutes, brushing steak with BBQ sauce. Turn steak, brush with BBQ sauce and broil another 8 minutes.

CHILI CASSEROLE   Bake 350° 20 Minutes

1. 1 Package (10 oz.) Tortilla Chips (coarsely broken)
2. 1 Can Nacho Cheese Soup (undiluted)
3. 1 Can (15 oz.) Chili with Beans

Place 2 cups chips in lightly greased 1-quart baking dish. Spread half of cheese soup over chips. Spread all of the chili over soup. Top with remaining cheese soup. Bake uncovered at 350° for 15 minutes. Sprinkle with remaining chips. Bake 5 minutes longer.

BEAN BOATS   Bake 375° 25 Minutes

1. 2 Cans (15 oz.) Chili with Beans
2. 4 French Rolls
3. 1/4 Cup Margarine (melted)
4. 1/2 Cup Shredded Cheddar Cheese

Cut tops off each french roll. Hollow out each roll reserving bread pieces. Brush inside and outside of rolls with margarine. Mix one cup of the bread pieces with chili and fill loaves. Replace tops of rolls and wrap in foil. Bake on cookie sheet at 375° for 25 minutes. Remove tops and sprinkle with cheese. Replace tops and serve hot.

FLANK STEAK SUPREME

Bake 350°
1 1/2 Hours

1. 1 Tenderized Flank Steak
2. Onion Salt
3. 1 Can (12 oz.) Mushroom Gravy

Preheat oven to 350°. Place steak on aluminum foil in casserole. Season with onion salt. Spread mushroom gravy over steak. Roll steak. Wrap with foil and seal. Bake for 1 1/2 hours.

CHILI STUFFED PEPPERS

Stove Top

1. 1 Can (15 oz.) Chili with Beans
2. 4 Small Red or Green Peppers
3. 1 Can (11 oz.) Mexican Style Corn (drained)
4. Tortilla Chips

Slice tops off of peppers. Remove inside and cook peppers gently in boiling water for 15 minutes. Drain. In a saucepan combine chili and corn and heat until boiling. Fill peppers and garnish with tortilla chips.

After removing a roast from the oven,
let it rest about 15 minutes
for easier carving.

BROCCOLI CHICKEN   Bake 350°   1 Hour

1. 6-8 Chicken Breasts (boneless, skinless)
2. 2 Packages (10 oz. each) Frozen Broccoil
3. 1 Can Nacho Cheese Soup
4. 1/4 Cup Cooking Sherry

In a skillet, brown chicken breasts and place in greased casserole. Mix broccoli, soup and sherry together. Pour over chicken and bake at 350° uncovered for 1 hour.

CLUB CHICKEN   Bake 375°   1 Hour

1. 1 Cup Club or Town House Crackers (finely crushed)
2. 1 Package Italian Salad Dressing Mix
3. 2-3 Pounds Frying Chicken
4. 3 Tablespoons Margarine (melted)

Combine cracker crumbs and salad dressing in large plastic bag. Shake 2 chicken pieces at a time in the crumb mixture. Place chicken, skin side up, in casserole dish. Drizzle with melted margarine. Bake for 1 hour at 375°.

CHICKEN RISOTTO   Stove Top

1. 2 1/2 Pounds Frying Chicken (cut up)
2. 1 Package (7 1/2 oz.) Rice-a-Roni (any flavor)
3. 1 Can Chicken Broth (plus water to equal 2 1/4 cups liquid)
4. 1 Jar (3 oz.) Pimiento Stuffed Olives (drained)

In a skillet, brown chicken (about 10 minutes on each side). Remove chicken from skillet leaving grease in pan. Add rice, including seasoning packet, to skillet and stir until lightly browned. Pour in chicken broth and water. Bring mixture to a boil. Place chicken on top of rice mixture. Lower heat, cover and simmer 20-30 minutes. Fluff rice with fork and top with olives.

CHERRY SHERRY CHICKEN   Bake 350°
                                         1 - 1 1/2 Hours

1. 4-6 Chicken Breasts
2. 2 Cups Cooking Sherry
3. 1 Can (16 oz.) Tart Pitted Cherries (drained)

Pour sherry and cherries over chicken pieces, cover and bake for 1 to 1 1/2 hours at 325°.

NUTTY CHICKEN   Bake 350°   1 Hour

1. 1 Cup Biscuit Mix (mixed in 1 cup water)
2. 1 Package (3.75 oz.) Salted Roasted Sunflower Nuts (chopped)
3. 3-4 Pounds Chicken Pieces
4. Vegetable Oil

Combine biscuit mix, water and nuts. Dip chicken in batter and brown in hot oil until golden. Place chicken in shallow baking dish and bake for 1 hour at 350°.

CHICKEN WILD RICE CASSEROLE   Bake 375°
45 Minutes

1. 1 Package (6 oz.) Wild Rice (cooked)
2. 2 Cups Chicken Meat (cooked, boned, cubed)
3. 2 Cans Cream of Mushroom Soup
4. 1/3 Cup Chicken Broth

Prepare rice as directed on package. Mix all the above ingredients and bake for 45 minutes at 375°.

SWISS CHICKEN CASSEROLE   Bake 350°
1 Hour

1. 6 Chicken Breasts (skinless, boneless)
2. 6 Slices Swiss Cheese
3. 1 Can Cream of Chicken Soup (undiluted)
4. 1/4 Cup Milk

Place chicken in greased casserole. Top with cheese. Mix soup and milk; stir well. Spoon over chicken and cover. Bake for 1 hour at 350°.

CHICKEN SPINACH BAKE   Bake 400°
15 Minutes

1. 1 Package (8 oz.) Fine Egg Noodles
2. 1 Package (9 oz.) Frozen Creamed Spinach (thawed)
3. 1 Tablespoon Vegetable Oil
4. 1 1/2 Cups Chicken (cooked, cubed)

Cook noodles and drain. Coat 9x9 baking dish with cooking spray. Turn noodles into dish and stir in spinach and oil. Top with chicken and bake for 15 minutes at 400°.

HONEY MUSTARD CHICKEN   Broil
8-10 Minutes Per Side

1. 1/2 Cup Miracle Whip Salad Dressing
2. 2 Tablespoons Dijon Mustard
3. 1 Tablespoon Honey
4. 4 Chicken Breasts (skinless, boneless)

Combine salad dressing, mustard and honey. Brush chicken with 1/2 of mixture and broil 8-10 minutes per side. After turning chicken, baste with remaining mixture.

To test chicken for doneness, pierce a meaty portion. Meat should be tender and moist with no pink tinge. Meat juices should be clear.

ITALIAN CHICKEN   Stove Top

1. 6-8 Chicken Breasts (skinless, boneless)
2. 2 Tablespoons Vegetable Oil
3. 1 Cup Chopped Onion
4. 1 Jar (14 oz.) Spaghetti Sauce With Mushrooms

Brown chicken in oil. Push to one side and saute onions until tender. Stir in spaghetti sauce and cover skillet. Simmer for 25 minutes or until chicken is tender. Serve with pasta.

ZESTY CRISP CHICKEN   Bake 350°   1 Hour

1. 4 Chicken Breasts (boneless, skinless)
2. 1 Egg (slightly beaten)
3. 1/4 Cup Soy Sauce
4. 1 1/4 Cup Corn Flakes (crushed)

Mix egg and soy sauce. Dip chicken pieces in soy sauce mixture. Coat with corn flake crumbs. Place on baking sheet and bake for 1 hour at 350°.

HERB LEMON CHICKEN   Stove Top

1. 4 Chicken Breasts (boneless, skinless)
2. 1 Egg (Beaten)
3. All Purpose Flour
4. 1 Package Lipton Golden Herb with Lemon Mix
   (mixed with 1-cup water)

Dip chicken in egg, then flour. Place in large skillet and brown in oil over medium heat. Add soup mix and bring to a boil. Cover and simmer 30 minutes or until chicken is cooked.

POTATO MUSTARD CHICKEN   Bake 400°
45 Minutes

1. 4 Chicken Breasts
2. 2 Cups Potatoes (shredded)
3. 1 Onion (sliced)
4. 1/2 Cup Honey Mustard Prepared Salad Dressing

Spread shredded potatoes in bottom of 9x12 lightly greased casserole. Place sliced onion on top of potatoes. Place chicken breasts on top of onions and drizzle salad dressing over chicken breasts. Bake 45 minutes at 400°. Season to taste.

FIESTA CHICKEN   Bake 350°
1 Hour

1. 4 Chicken Breasts (boneless, skinless)
2. 1/2 Cup Yogurt
3. 2 Tablespoons Taco Seasoning Mix
4. 1 Cup Cheddar Cheese Cracker Crumbs

Coat chicken breasts with yogurt. Combine cracker crumbs and taco seasoning. Dredge chicken in mixture. Place in greased baking dish. Bake uncovered 350° for 1 hour.

For quick seasoning while cooking, keep a
large shaker containing six parts salt
to one part pepper.

ONION RING CHICKEN   Bake 350° 45 Minutes

1. 4 Chicken Breasts (skinless, boneless)
2. 1/2 Cup Margarine (melted)
3. 1 Tablespoon Worcestershire Sauce
4. 1 Can (2.5 oz.) Fried Onion Rings (crushed)

Flatten each breast, season to taste. Combine margarine and worcestershire sauce. Dredge chicken in margarine mixure, then crushed onion rings. Arrange in baking pan. Top with any remaining margarine mixture. Bake at 350° for 45 minutes or until tender.

PECAN CHICKEN   Bake 350°   1 Hour

1. 1/4 Cup Honey
2. 1/4 Cup Dijon Mustard
3. 4 Chicken Breasts (skinned, boned, halved)
4. 1 Cup Pecans (finely ground)

Combine honey and mustard. Spread on both sides of chicken. Dredge chicken in chopped pecans. Place in lightly greased baking dish. Bake at 350° for 1 hour or until tender.

CONFETTI CHICKEN   Stove Top

1. 1 1/2 Cups Chicken (cooked and cubed)
2. 2 Cans (14 1/2 oz. each) Seasoned Tomatoes/ Onions
3. 1 Green Pepper (chopped)
4. 2 Cups Rice (cooked)

In skillet, combine first three ingredients and season to taste. Simmer for 10-15 minutes. Serve over rice.

TANGY CHICKEN   Stove Top

1. 2 1/2 Pounds Chicken (cut-up)
2. 2 Tablespoons Margarine
3. 1/2 Cup Heinz 57 Sauce
4. 1/2 Cup Water

In skillet, brown chicken in margarine. Combine sauce and water and pour over chicken. Cover and simmer for 40 minutes or until chicken is tender. Baste occasionally. Remove cover last 10 minutes of cooking. Spoon sauce over chicken before serving.

BAKED CHICKEN AND BEANS   Bake 350°
                                    50 Minutes

1. 4 Chicken Breasts
2. 1 Can Cream of Mushroom Soup
3. 1 Can (12 oz.) Cut Green Beans (drained)
4. 1 Package (16 oz.) Frozen Onion Rings

Place chicken in greased casserole and cover with soup. Bake for 30 minutes at 350°.   Place beans in casserole with chicken. Top with onion rings. Bake for 20 minutes longer or until chicken is tender and onion rings are crisp and brown.

CHICKEN NOODLE CASSEROLE Bake 350°
1 Hour

1. 1 Package (8 oz.) Egg Noodles (cooked, drained)
2. 1 Can Cream of Mushroom Soup (undiluted)
3. 6 Chicken Legs or Thighs
4. Paprika

Combine cooked noodles and soup. Place into a casserole. Arrange chicken on top of noodles. Sprinkle with paprika. Cover and bake at 350° for 1 hour or until chicken is tender.

HAWAIIAN CHICKEN Stove Top

1. 10 Ounces Breaded Chicken Tenders
2. 1 Jar (10 oz.) Sweet and Sour Sauce
3. 1 Can (8 3/4 oz.) Pineapple Tidbits
4. 1 Package (16 oz.) Frozen Oriental Vegetables

Prepare chicken tenders according to package directions. Place tenders in large skillet. Add sweet and sour sauce, pineapple and vegetables. Cover and simmer 25 minutes or until vegetables are tender. Serve over rice.

CHICKEN MEATBALLS   Stove Top

1. 1 Pound Ground Chicken
2. 1 Egg (slightly beaten)
3. 2/3 Cup Corn Bread Stuffing Mix
4. 2 Tablespoons Sour Cream

Combine chicken, egg and stuffing mix. Shape into
16 meatballs. Lightly coat skillet with cooking spray
and brown meatballs. Reduce heat to low and add
1/4 cup water. Cover and simmer for 15 minutes. Stir
a little cooking liquid into sour cream and then stir back
into skillet. Gently heat to serving temperature. Add
2 to 4 more tablespoons water, if necessary.

TURKEY ROLL-UPS   Stove Top
Bake 350°   25-30 Minutes

1. 1 Box (6 oz.) Stove Top Dressing
2. 1/4 Cup Margarine plus 1 2/3 Cups Water
3. 6 Slices "Deli" Turkey (medium thickness)
4. 1 Can (12 oz.) Chicken Gravy

Prepare dressing mix as directed with margarine and
water. Spoon dressing onto slice of turkey and roll up.
Place seam side down in casserole. Repeat until all
slices are "stuffed". Pour gravy over the top of turkey
and dressing. Bake for 25-30 minutes at 350°.

SPICY CHOPS   Broil

1. 4 Boneless Pork Loin Chops (1/2-inch thick)
2. 1/4 Cup Picante
3. 2 Tablespoons Water
4. 2 Tablespoons Marmalade

Place pork chops in baking dish. Mix picante, water and marmalade. Pour over chops, turning to coat. Marinate about 1 hour. Broil chops about 8-10 minutes per side, basting with leftover marinade.

PORK CHOPS WITH RED CABBAGE   Stove Top

1. 4 Loin Pork Chops (cut 1-inch thick)
2. 1 Large Onion (chopped)
3. 1 Jar (15 oz.) Sweet/Sour Red Cabbage
4. 1 Apple (quartered, cored, sliced)

Brown pork chops in non stick skillet. Remove chops. Saute onion until tender. Arrange chops over onions. Place cabbage and apple slices over top of pork chops. Cover and simmer for 30 minutes or until chops are cooked thoroughly.

The main rule to keep in mind when cooking pork is to cook it thoroughly.

PORK STIR FRY   Stove Top

1. 2 Boneless Pork Loin Chops (cut into 1/4-inch strips)
2. 1 Bag (14 oz.) Frozen Oriental Stir-Fry Vegetables/ Seasoning Pack
3. 1 Tablespoon Soy Sauce
4. 2 Teaspoons Vegetable Oil

Coat large skillet with cooking spray. Heat to medium high temperature and add pork strips. Stir-fry 3 minutes or until no longer pink. Add vegetables, cover and cook 5 minutes. Add 1/4 cup water, vegetable seasoning packet, soy sauce and oil. Cook, stirring until mixture is heated through. Serve over rice.

SAUCY PORK CHOPS   Bake 350°   1 Hour

1. 6 Pork Chops
2. 1 Cup Applesauce
3. 1/4 Cup Soy Sauce
4. 1/8 Teaspoon Onion Powder

Brown pork chops on both sides. Place in shallow casserole. Combine remaining ingredients and spoon evenly over chops. Cover and bake at 350° for 45 minutes. Remove cover and continue baking 15 minutes longer or until chops are tender.

PORK CHOP CASSEROLE SUPPER   Bake 350°
1 Hour

1. 4 Pork Chops
2. 1 Can (16 oz.) Peas
3. 1 Can Cream of Mushroom Soup
4. 1/4 Cup Onion (chopped)

Arrange pork chops in casserole. Combine peas, 1/4 cup of the pea liquid, soup and onion. Pour over pork chops and cover. Bake 50 minutes at 350°, uncover and bake an additional 10 minutes.

OVEN FRIED PORK CHOPS   Bake 425°
30-45 Minutes

1. 3 Tablespoons Margarine (melted)
2. 1 Egg plus 2 Tablespoons Water (beaten)
3. 1 Cup Cornbread Stuffing Mix
4. 4 Pork Chops

Place margarine in 13x9-inch baking pan. Dip pork chops in egg mixture, then stuffing mix to coat. Place chops on top of melted margarine. Bake for 20 minutes at 425°, turn and bake 10-15 minutes more or until browned.

TEX MEX CHOPS   Stove Top

1. 4 Boneless Pork Chops
2. 1 Tablespoon Vegetable Oil
3. 1 Cup Salsa

Season pork chops to taste. In skillet, brown both sides
of chops in oil. Add salsa and lower heat. Simmer
30 minutes or until chops are thoroughly cooked.

MUSTARD-APRICOT PORK CHOPS   Broil

1. 1/3 Cup Apricot Preserves
2. 2 Tablespoons Dijon Mustard
3. 4 (3/4-inch) Pork Chops
4. 3 Green Onions (chopped)

Combine preserves and mustard in small saucepan.
Heat until preserves melt, stirring. Set aside. Place
chops on lightly greased broiler pan. Broil 5 minutes.
Brush chops with half of the glaze and turn. Broil
5 minutes longer. Turn and brush with remaining
glaze. Broil 2 minutes. Garnish with green onions
before serving.

GRILLED PORK CHOPS   Grill

1. 1/4 Teaspoon Salt
2. 3/4 Teaspoon Lemon Pepper
3. 1/2 Teaspoon Dried Whole Oregano Leaves
4. 4 (1-inch thick) Pork Chops

Mix salt, lemon pepper and oregano. Coat pork chops.
Grill over low to medium hot heat for 25 minutes or
until chops are no longer pink. Turn once.

HONEY GLAZED HAM   Bake 325°   2 1/2 Hours

1. 10 Pound Ham
2. 1/2 Cup Honey
3. 1/3 Cup Brown Sugar
4. 1/4 Cup Orange Juice

Score ham. Mix honey, brown sugar and orange juice together. Rub mixture over scored ham and place fat side up in roasting pan. Bake at 325° for 2 1/2 hours. Last 30 minutes, baste with juices.

HAM IN MADEIRA WINE   Stove Top

1. 10 Pound Ham
2. 4 Bay Leaves
3. 8 Peppercorns
4. 1 Bottle Madeira Wine

Soak ham in cold water overnight. Drain. In large pot, cover drained ham in boiling water. Add bay leaves and peppercorns and cook slowly 2 1/2 hours. Drain off liquid. Pour wine over ham and simmer at least 1/2 hour, basting with wine. Slice and serve.

OVEN BRAISED HAM   Bake 350° 30 Minutes

1. 6 Slices Cooked Ham (1/4-inch thick)
2. 2 Tablespoons Brown Sugar
3. 1/4 Cup Water

Place ham in lightly greased casserole. Sprinkle with brown sugar. Pour water around ham. Cover and bake at 350° for 30 minutes.

HAM WITH RED-EYE GRAVY   Stove Top

1. 6 Slices Country Ham (1/4-inch thick)
2. 1/4 Cup Margarine
3. 1/4 Cup Firmly Packed Brown Sugar
4. 1/2 Cup Strong Black Coffee

Saute ham in margarine over low heat until light brown,
turning several times. Remove ham from skillet, cover
with foil to keep warm. Stir sugar into pan drippings
and heat until sugar dissolves, stirring constantly. Add
coffee and simmer 5 minutes. Season gravy to taste.
Serve over ham slices.

ROMAN SPAGHETTI   Stove Top

1. 1/2 Pound Lean Bacon (diced)
2. 1/4 Cup Margarine
3. 1 Pound Spaghetti Noodles (cooked, drained)
4. 2/3 Cup Romano Cheese

Melt margarine in saucepan and cook bacon until crisp.
Remove bacon, retain bacon grease and margarine.
Place spaghetti in serving bowl. Toss half of the bacon
grease/margarine mixture with the spaghetti. Sprinkle
with bacon and cheese and serve.

SAUSAGE BAKE   Bake 350° 45 Minutes

1. 1 Pound Polish Sausage (cut 1-inch pieces)
2. 1 Cup Cheese (shredded)
3. 1 Cup Celery (sliced)
4. 2 Cans (10 3/4 oz.) Cream of Mushroom Soup

Combine all ingredients and place in 2 quart casserole.
Bake covered 45 minutes at 350°.

FRANKS AND CRESCENTS   Bake 375°
                                       10-12 Minutes

1. 8 Hot Dogs (partially split along length)
2. Cheddar Cheese (cut in strips)
3. 1 Can (8 oz.) Refrigerated Crescent Dinner Rolls

Fill each hot dog with strip of cheese. Separate
crescent dough into 8 triangles. Place hot dog on each
triangle and roll up. Place on greased cookie sheet
(cheese side up) and bake at 375° for 10-12 minutes.

HOT DOG TACOS   Stove Top

1. 4 Hot Dogs (finely chopped)
2. 2 Ounces Velveeta Cheese (cubed)
3. 1/3 Cup Picante
4. Flour Tortillas (warmed)

Place first 3 ingredients in non-stick skillet. Heat over
low heat until cheese is melted. Place mixture in flour
tortilla and roll up.

BAKED ORANGE ROUGHY

Bake 400°
25 Minutes

1. 1 Pound Orange Roughy Fillets
2. 1/4 Cup Lemon Juice
3. 1/2 Teaspoon Tarragon Leaves
4. 2 Teaspoons Dried Mustard

Place fillets in large casserole. Squeeze lemon juice over fillets. Sprinkle dried mustard and tarragon leaves over fish. Bake at 400° for 25 minutes.

BUTTERMILK FRIED FILLETS

Stove Top

1. 2 Pounds Skinless Fish Fillets
2. 1 Cup Buttermilk
3. 1 Cup Bisquick Mix
4. Cooking Oil

Place fish in shallow dish. Pour buttermilk over fish and let it marinate for 30 minutes, turning once. Roll fish in bisquick mix, season to taste and fry in hot oil 4-5 minutes on each side.

You should not thaw fish at room
temperature or in warm water. It will lose
moisture and flavor. Instead, thaw fish
in the refrigerator.

SPANISH FISH   Bake 350° 20 Minutes Per Pound

1. 1 Fish (Snapper, Redfish)
2. 1 Bell Pepper (chopped)
3. 1 Red Onion (chopped)
4. 1 Can (14 1/2 oz.) Seasoned Tomatoes

Line shallow pan with foil leaving ample amount hanging over the edges. Pour 1/3 of the tomatoes onto the foil. Place fish over tomatoes. Sprinkle the bell pepper and onion over the fish. Pour remaining tomatoes over fish and loosely close up foil. Bake at 350° for 20 minutes per pound or until fish is flakey.

CORDON BLEU FISH FILLETS   Bake 400°
2-3 Minutes

1. 1 Package (8 oz.) Fried Fish Fillets
2. 4 Slices Boiled Ham
3. 4 Slices Swiss Cheese
4. 1 Can Cream of Mushroom Soup (plus 1/2 Soup Can Water)

Prepare fish according to package directions. Top each cooked fillet with a slice of ham and cheese. Return to 400° oven for 2-3 minutes until cheese is partially melted. Combine soup and water in small saucepan and heat thoroughly. Pour over fish and serve.

CAESAR'S FISH   Bake 400°   15 Minutes

1. 1 Pound Flounder Fillets
2. 1/2 Cup Prepared Caesar's Salad Dressing
3. 1 Cup Round Buttery Cracker Crumbs
4. 1/2 Cup Shredded Cheddar Cheese

Place fillets in lightly greased casserole dish. Drizzle
Caesar dressing over fillets. Sprinkle cracker crumbs
over top of fillets. Bake at 400° for 10 minutes. Top
with cheese and bake an additional 5 minutes or until
fish flakes easily with fork.

LEMON DILL FISH   Broil
                               5-8 Minutes Per Side

1. 1 Pound Fish Fillets
2. 1/2 Cup Miracle Whip
3. 2 Tablespoons Lemon Juice
4. 1 Teaspoon Dillweed

Combine Miracle Whip, lemon juice and dill. Place
fish in broiler pan. Brush with sauce. Broil 5-8
minutes, turn once and brush with sauce.
Continuing broiling for 5-8 minutes.

As a rule, thawed fish should not be kept
longer than one day before cooking. The
flavor is better if it is cooked
immediately after thawing.

TROUT ALMANDINE   Bake 350°   25 Minutes

1. 2 Trout Fillets
2. 1/3 Cup Slivered Almonds
3. 1 Tablespoon Butter (melted)
4. 1/2 Teaspoon Chopped Parsley

Arrange almonds on ungreased cookie sheet and bake
for 4-5 minutes at 350°. Set aside. Place fish on
ungreased baking sheet. Combine almonds, butter and
parsley. Spoon over fish. Bake uncovered at 350° for
25 minutes.

ITALIAN SCALLOPS   Stove Top

1. 1 Tablespoon Butter
2. 1 Tablespoon Garlic Powder
3. 1/2 Tablespoon Italian Herbs
4. 1 Pound Fresh Sea Scallops

Melt butter in large skillet. Add garlic powder, scallops
and Italian herbs. Cook over medium-high heat,
stirring constantly, 6-8 minutes.

PEPPER SHRIMP   Bake 350°   30 Minutes

1. 1 Pound Jumbo Shrimp in Shells
2. 1/2 Cup Butter (melted)
3. 3 Tablespoons Worcestershire Sauce
4. 3 Tablespoons Fresh Ground Pepper

Arrange shrimp in one layer in flat pan. Combine
butter, worcestershire sauce and pepper. Pour sauce
mixture over shrimp and stir. Bake uncovered at 350°
for 30 minutes. Stir often.

MARINATED GRILLED SHRIMP   Grill or Broil

1. 2 Tablespoons Soy Sauce
2. 2 Tablespoons Vegetable Oil
3. 1 Tablespoon Honey
4. 1 Pound Large Shrimp (peeled, deveined)

Mix soy sauce, oil and honey and pour over shrimp.
Marinate at least one hour. Place on skewers and grill
or broil 4-5 minutes until cooked through and browned.

SHRIMP MARINARA   Stove Top

1. 1 Clove Garlic (minced)
2. 1 Tablespoon Vegetable Oil
3. 1 Can (1 lb. 12 oz.) Italian Style Tomatoes
4. 1 Pound Frozen Shrimp (shelled, deveined)

Saute garlic in oil until tender. Add tomatoes and cook
until sauce thickens and tomatoes break up, about 20
minutes. Add shrimp and cook 5 more minutes. Serve
over rice.

EASY CRAB DISH   Broil   12-15 Minutes

1. 1 Pound Lump Blue Crab Meat (fresh or frozen)
2. 1/2 Cup Margarine (melted)
3. 1 Tablespoon Vinegar
4. 1 Teaspoon Tarragon

Thaw frozen crab meat. Drain. Place crab meat in
shallow casserole. Combine margarine and vinegar and
pour over crab. Sprinkle with tarragon. Toss. Broil
12-15 minutes or until lightly browned.

BACON CRISP OYSTERS

Broil

1. 1 Jar (12 oz.) Fresh Oysters (drained)
2. 8 Slices Bacon (cut into thirds)
3. 2 Tablespoons Parsley
4. Salt/Pepper

Place one oyster on each piece of bacon. Sprinkle with parsley, salt and pepper. Wrap bacon around oyster and secure with toothpick. Place broiler rack 4 inches from heat and broil 8 minutes on one side. Turn and broil 5 minutes on other side. Bacon will be crisp and oysters will curl.

OYSTER SAUSAGE STEW

Stove Top

1. 1/2 Pound Pork Sausage
2. 1/2 Cup Onion (diced)
3. 1 Container (12 oz.) Fresh Oysters
4. 1 1/2 Cup Milk

Brown sausage and onion. Remove from skillet. Place oysters with liquid in skillet and cook over low heat until edges curl. Turn. Return sausage and onion to skillet. Stir in milk. Simmer until thoroughly heated.

GRILLED TUNA STEAKS
Grill or Broil
5 Minutes Per Side

1. 4 Tuna Steaks
2. 1 Cup Prepared Italian Salad Dressing
3. 2 Teaspoons Fresh Ground Pepper
4. 1 Lemon

Place steaks in casserole. Pour dressing over tuna.
Cover and refrigerate for 1 hour, turning once. Remove
steaks from marinade and sprinkle pepper on both
sides. Grill or broil 5 minutes on each side. Squeeze
lemon over steaks and serve.

QUICK TUNA CASSEROLE
Bake 350°
20 Minutes

1. 1 Can (6 1/2 oz.) Tuna (drained)
2. 3 Cups Rice Krispies
3. 1 Can Cream of Mushroom Soup
4. 1 Can Chicken Noodle Soup

Mix above ingredients and bake at 350° for 20 minutes.

BROCCOLI TUNA CASSEROLE
Bake 350°
1 Hour

1. 1 Can (6 1/2 oz.) Tuna (drained)
2. 1 Package (10 oz.) Frozen Chopped Broccoli
   (thawed, drained)
3. 1 Can Mushroom Soup
4. 1 Cup Crushed Seasoned Potato Chips

Layer tuna, broccoli and mushroom soup in small
baking dish. Cover with crushed potato chips. Bake,
uncovered, at 350° for 1 hour.

TATER TOT TUNA   Bake 300°   20 Minutes

1. 2 Cans (6 1/2 oz. each) Tuna (drained)
2. 1 Can Cream of Chicken Soup
3. 1 Can (16 oz.) French-style Green Beans (drained)
4. 1 Package (16 oz.) Tater Tots

Combine tuna with soup and green beans. Place in casserole dish. Brown tater-tots in oven according to package directions. Place tater-tots on top of tuna mixture. Bake at 300° for 20 minutes or until mixture is bubbly.

QUICK TUNA POT PIE   Bake 425°   15 Minutes

1. 1 Can (6 1/2 oz.) Tuna (drained)
2. 1 Can Mushroom Soup
3. 1 Can (16 oz.) Peas (drained)
4. 1 Can Refrigerator Biscuits

Combine tuna, soup and peas. Place in greased casserole. Arrange biscuits on top of mixture. Bake at 425° for 15 minutes or until biscuits are golden brown.

DESSERTS

PINEAPPLE-LEMON PIE - Graham Cracker Crust

1. 1 Can (6 oz.) Frozen Lemonaide
2. 1 Can (14 oz.) Sweetened Condensed Milk
3. 1 Carton (8 oz.) Cool Whip
4. 1 Can (15 1/4 oz.) Crushed Pineapple (drained)

Mix above ingredients and pour into graham cracker crust. Freeze until ready to serve.

BLUEBERRY PIE - Graham Cracker Crust

1. 1 Can (1 lb. 6 oz.) Blueberry Pie Filling
2. 1 Carton (8 oz.) Cool Whip
3. 1 Package (8 oz.) Cream Cheese (softened)

Place pie filling in graham cracker crust. Combine softened cream cheese with Cool Whip and spread over pie filling. Chill at least one hour before serving.

KEY LIME PIE - Unbaked Pie Shell

1. 6 Egg Yolks
2. 2 Cans (14 oz. each) Sweetened Condensed Milk
3. 1 Cup Realime Lime Juice from Concentrate
4. Green Food Coloring (optional)

Combine and beat above ingredients. Pour into pie shell. Bake at 325° for 40 minutes. Cool and chill in refrigerator before serving.

MARGARITA PIE - Graham Cracker Crust

1. 1 Package (8 oz.) Cream Cheese (softened)
2. 2 Packages Holland House Margarita Mix
3. 1/2 to 3/4 Cup Sugar
4. 1 Carton (8 oz.) Cool Whip

Cream the cream cheese until fluffy. Add margarita mix and sugar and beat until smooth. Add Cool Whip and mix. Freeze in graham cracker crust until ready to serve.

KOOLAIDE PIE - Graham Cracker Crust

1. 1 Can (12 oz.) Evaporated Milk (refrigerated so it is cold)
2. 2/3 Cup Sugar
3. 1 Package (.15 oz.) Koolade (any flavor)

Beat milk until it is doubled in size. Add sugar and koolaide and beat until thickened (about 5 minutes). Place in graham cracker crust and refrigerate until ready to serve.

VANILLA SOUR CREAM PIE - Baked Pie Shell

1. 1 Cup Sour Cream
2. 1 Cup Milk
3. 1 Package (3 1/2 oz.) Vanilla Instant Pudding

Beat sour cream and milk until smooth. Beat in dry pudding mix until smooth and slightly thickened. Pour into pie crust and chill 1 hour or until set.

COOKIE CRUST ICE CREAM PIE

1. 1 Roll (18 oz.) Refrigerator Chocolate Chip Cookies
2. 1 Quart Chocolate Ice Cream (softened)
3. 1 Jar (12 oz.) Chocolate Fudge Sauce
4. 1 Carton (8 oz.) Cool Whip

Slice cookie dough 1/8-inch thick. Line bottom and sides of 9-inch pie pan with cookie slices, overlapping sides to make scalloped edge. Bake 10 minutes at 375°. Cool. Fill cooled crust with ice cream. Top with syrup and frost with Cool Whip. Freeze. To serve, cut into wedges.

BUTTER PECAN PIE   Graham Cracker Crust

1. 1 1/2 Cups Butter Pecan Ice Cream (softened)
2. 2 (1 1/2 oz. each) English Toffee Flavored Candy Bars (crushed)
3. 1 1/2 Cups Vanilla Ice Cream (softened)

Spread Butter Pecan Ice Cream in graham cracker crust. Sprinkle with half of crushed candy bar. Freeze. Spread vanilla ice cream over top of crushed candy bar. Sprinkle with remaining candy and freeze until ready to serve.

PEANUT BUTTER PIE - Graham Cracker Crust

1. 1 Package (8 oz.) Cream Cheese (softened)
2. 1 Cup Powdered Sugar
3. 1 Cup Crunchy Peanut Butter
4. 1 Carton (8 oz.) Cool Whip

Cream the cream cheese. Add sugar and peanut butter.
Beat until smooth. Fold in Cool Whip. Place in
graham cracker crust. Refrigerate or freeze.

STRAWBERRY PIE - Baked Pie Shell

1. 1 Tablespoon Strawberry Jello plus 1 Cup Hot Water
2. 3 Tablespoons Cornstarch
3. 1 Cup Sugar
4. 1 Pint Fresh Strawberries (sliced)

Mix first three ingredients in saucepan and cook over
medium heat until thick. Remove from heat and stir in
strawberries. Cool. Pour into baked pie shell. Refrigerate.

STRAWBERRY MALLOW PIE   Baked Pie Shell

1. 1 Package (10 oz.) Frozen Sweetened Strawberries
   (thawed)
2. 20 Large Marshmallows
3. 1 Carton (8 oz.) Cool Whip

Pour strawberry juice in pan and heat slowly adding
marshmallows. Stir until marshmallows are melted.
Cool. Fold in Cool Whip and strawberries. Mix well.
Pour into pie shell and refrigerate.

STRAWBERRY YOGURT PIE

Graham Cracker Crust

1. 2 Cups Strawberry Yogurt
2. 1/2 Cup Strawberry Preserves
3. 1 Carton (8 oz.) Cool Whip (thawed)

Combine strawberry preserves and yogurt in bowl. Fold in Cool Whip. Spoon into graham cracker crust and freeze. Remove and place in refrigerator for 30 minutes before serving.

GERMAN CHOCOLATE PIE

Baked Chocolate Pie Shell

1. 1 Package (4 oz.) Baker's German Sweet Chocolate
2. 1/3 Cup Milk
3. 1 Package (3 oz.) Cream Cheese (softened)
4. 1 Carton (8 oz.) Cool Whip

Heat chocolate and 2 tablespoons milk over low heat. Stir until melted. Remove from heat. Beat cream cheese and add remaining milk and chocolate mixture. Beat until smooth. Fold Cool Whip into chocolate mixture and blend until smooth. Spoon into crust. Freeze about 4 hours before serving.

> Frozen unbaked pie shells do not need to be thawed and can go right into oven.

MALTED MILK PIE - Baked Graham Cracker Crust

1. 1 Pint Vanilla Ice Cream (softened)
2. 1 1/2 Cups Malted Milk Balls (crushed)
3. 1 Carton (8 oz.) Cool Whip
4. 1/3 Cup Marshmallow Topping

Combine ice cream with 1/2 cup crushed malted milk balls. Spread mixture into graham cracker crust. Freeze. Blend marshmallow topping with 3/4 cup crushed malted milk balls. Fold into Cool Whip. Spread over frozen ice cream layer. Freeze several hours. Top with remaining 1/4 cup crushed malt balls.

ANGEL NUT CAKE

1. 7 Egg Whites
2. 1 1/2 Cup Ground Nuts
3. 1 1/2 Cups Powdered Sugar (sifted)

Beat egg whites until stiff. Fold in nuts and sugar. Bake in greased tube pan or flat cake pan for about 45 minutes at 350°. See Angel Nut Frosting.

ANGEL NUT FROSTING

1. 5 Tablespoons Milk
2. 1 Cup Sugar
3. 5 Tablespoons Butter
4. 1/2 Cup Chocolate Chips

In saucepan, melt butter; add sugar and milk. Bring to a boil, stir one minute or until slightly thick. Fold in chocolate chips. Frost cake.

BUTTER CAKE

1. 1 Cup Butter (softened)
2. 2 Cups Flour
3. 1 Cup Sugar
4. 1 Egg (slightly beaten)

Mix ingredients. Place dough in greased and floured round cake pan. Bake at 375° for 30 minutes. Serve warm with fresh fruit.

LEMON CAKE

1. 1 Package Lemon Pudding Cake Mix
2. 2/3 Cup Oil
3. 4 Eggs
4. 1 1/4 Cups 7-Up

Mix cake and oil. Beat. Add eggs one at a time. Add 7-Up; beat. Pour into a greased and floured 13x9-inch cake pan. Bake at 350° for 30 minutes.

LEMON CAKE FROSTING

1. 1 Carton (8 oz.) Cool Whip
2. 1 Can (8 oz.) Crushed Pineapple (drained)
3. 1 Cup Coconut

Mix above ingredients and frost cake. Refrigerate until ready to serve.

TOMATO SPICE CAKE

1. 1 Package Spice Cake Mix
2. 1 Can (10 oz.) Tomato Soup plus 1/4 Cup Water
3. 3 eggs
4. 1/3 Cup Vegetable Oil

Combine ingredients in large bowl. Beat at low spead until moistened. Beat at medium speed for 2 minutes. Pour batter into 9x13-inch cake pan and bake at 350° for 30-35 minutes.

RICH CHOCOLATE CAKE

1. 1 Package Devil's Food Cake Mix
2. 3 Eggs
3. 1 1/3 Cup Water
4. 1 Cup Miracle Whip

Mix above ingredients. Place in greased 9x13-inch cake pan. Bake at 350° for 40 minutes.

Cake tip - for best results in cake baking, let eggs, butter and milk reach room temperature before mixing.

UGLY DUCKLING CAKE

1. 1 Box Yellow Cake Mix
2. 1 Can (17 oz.) Fruit Cocktail With Syrup
3. 1 Cup Coconut
4. 2 Eggs

Blend above ingredients. Beat 2 minutes at medium speed. Pour into a greased 9x13-inch cake pan. Bake at 350° for 45 minutes.

UGLY DUCKLY FROSTING

1. 1 Cup Brown Sugar
2. 1/4 Cup Evaporated Milk
3. 1 Stick Margarine
4. 1 Cup Coconut

In sauce pan, combine brown sugar, milk and margarine. Cook 5 minutes over medium heat, stirring constantly. Remove from heat and stir in coconut. Pour over cake.

FESTIVE CRANBERRY CAKE

1. 1 Angel Food Cake (prepared)
2. 1 1/2 Cups Chilled Whipping Cream
3. 1/3 Cup Confectioners Sugar
4. 1 Jar (14 oz.) Cranberry-Orange Relish

Split cake to make 4 layers. In chilled bowl, beat whipping cream and sugar until stiff. Stack layers spreading each with a fourth of the whipped cream mixture, then a fourth of the cranberry-orange relish. Swirl it into whipped cream. Refrigerate cake 1 to 2 hours before serving.

TRIPLE FUDGE CAKE

1. 1 Package (4 oz.) Chocolate Pudding and Pie Filling
2. 2 Cups Milk
3. 1 Package Devils Food Cake Mix
4. 1/2 Cup Semisweet Chocolate Chips

Cook chocolate pudding in 2 cups milk. Blend cake mix
into hot pudding, beating by hand or with mixer for
2 minutes. Pour into greased and floured 9x13-inch cake
pan. Sprinkle batter with chocolate chips. Bake at 350°
for 35 minutes. If desired, top with whipped cream.

APRICOT CAKE

1. 1 Yellow Cake Mix
2. 4 Egg Whites
3. 1/2 Cup Canola Oil
4. 1 Cup Apricot Nectar

Spray bundt pan with vegetable spray. Mix above
ingredients and pour into pan. Bake at 350° for
30 minutes. Best if it is slightly undercooked.

ALMOND BARK COOKIES

1. 1 Package (24 oz.) Almond Bark
2. 1 Cup Peanut Butter
3. 8 Cups Captain Krunch Cereal
4. 1 Cup Salted Peanuts

Melt almond bark according to package directions. Add
peanut butter and mix. Remove from heat and stir in cereal
and peanuts. Drop by spoonfuls onto wax paper. Cool.

COCONUT COOKIES

1. 1 Package (14 oz.) Coconut
2. 1 Package (12 oz.) Semi-sweet Chocolate Chips
3. 1 Can (14 oz.) Sweetened Condensed Milk

Mix ingredients. Drop by tablespoonful onto lightly greased cookie sheet. Bake at 325° for 13-15 minutes.

LEMON WHIPPERSNAPS

1. 1 Package Lemon Cake Mix with Pudding
2. 2 Cups Cool Whip (thawed)
3. 1 Egg (slightly beaten)
4. 1/2 Cup Sifted Powder Sugar

Combine first 3 ingredients. Stir until mixture is uniformly moist. Form into small balls. Roll balls into powdered sugar and place on lightly greased cookie sheet. Bake in preheated oven for 10-12 minutes at 350°.

ORANGE COCONUT BALLS

1. 3 Cups Finely Crushed Vanilla Wafers
2. 2 Cups Flaked Coconut
3. 1 Cup Pecans (finely chopped)
4. 1 Can (6 oz.) Orange Juice Concentrate (thawed)

Combine ingredients and shape into bite-sized balls. If desired, roll in crushed vanilla wafer crumbs. Refrigerate in airtight container.

FUDGE COOKIES

1. 1 Package Devil's Food Cake Mix
2. 2 Eggs
3. 1/2 Cup Oil
4. 1 Cup Semi-sweet Chocolate Chips

Mix cake mix, eggs and oil. Stir in chocolate chips.
Mixture will be stiff. Shape dough into small balls.
Place 2 inches apart on cookie sheet and bake at 350°
for 10-12 minutes.

GOLD BROWNIES

1. 2 Cups Graham Cracker Crumbs
2. 1 Can (14 oz.) Sweetened Condensed Milk
3. 1 Package (6 oz.) Chocolate Chips
4. 1/2 Cup Pecans (chopped)

Mix together and place in 8x8-inch greased pan. Bake
for 30 minutes at 350°. Cool. Cut into squares and
remove from pan.

PEANUT BUTTER CANDY COOKIES

1. 1/2 Cup Peanut Butter
2. 1/2 Cup Sugar
3. 1/4 Cup Evaporated Milk
4. 2 1/2 Cups Cornflakes

Mix peanut butter, sugar and milk into a smooth cream.
Stir in cornflakes until thoroughly blended. Drop by
teaspoonful onto ungreased cookie sheet. Bake at 375°
for 6 minutes or until evenly browned.

RAISIN TREATS

1. 1/4 Cup Margarine
2. 1 Package (10 oz.) Marshmallows
3. 1 Cup Raisins
4. 5 Cups Rice Krispies

Melt margarine over low heat in double boiler. Add marshmallows and stir until completely melted. Cook over low heat 3 minutes, stirring constantly. Remove from heat and add cereal and raisins. Stir until well coated. Pour and press mixture evenly into buttered 9x13-inch cake pan. Cut into squares when cool.

LEMON COOKIES

1. 1 Lemon Cake Mix
2. 1 Stick Margarine (softened)
3. 1 Package (8 oz.) Cream Cheese (softened)
4. 1 Egg

Mix above ingredients, blending well. Drop by teaspoonful onto lightly greased cookie sheet. Bake at 375° for 10-12 minutes.

Cookie tip - let cookies cool completely before storing. To keep cookies fresh, store soft and chewy ones in an airtight container. Crisp cookies in a jar with a loose fitting lid.

CHOCOLATE MARSHMALLOW SLICES

1. 1 Package (12 oz.) Semi-sweet Chocolate Chips
2. 1/2 Cup Margarine
3. 6 Cups (10 1/2 oz.) Miniature Marshmallows
4. 1 Cup Pecans (finely chopped)

In saucepan, melt chocolate chips and margarine over low heat. Stir constantly until blended. Remove from heat, cool for 5 minutes. Stir in marshmallows and nuts. Do not melt marshmallows. On wax paper, shape mixture into 2 rolls, 2 inches in diameter. Wrap rolls in wax paper and chill overnight. Cut rolls into 1/4-inch slices. Store in airtight container until ready to serve.

CHOCOLATE PEANUT CLUSTERS

1. 1/2 Cup Milk Chocolate Chips
2. 1/2 Cup Semi-Sweet Chocolate Chips
3. 1 Tablespoon Shortening
4. 1 Cup Unsalted, Roasted Peanuts

Melt first three ingredients in double boiler, stirring until smooth. Remove from heat and stir in peanuts. Drop by teaspoonfuls into 1-inch diameter candy papers or onto wax paper. Allow to set until firm and store in airtight container.

CHOCOLATE BITES

1. 1 Package (6 oz.) Semi-Sweet Chocolate Chips
2. 1/2 Cup Peanut Butter
3. 1/2 Cup Margarine
4. 8 Cups Rice Chex

Combine first 3 ingredients in saucepan. Cook over low heat until chips melt. Stir occasionally. Remove from heat and stir. Pour over cereal and stir to coat evenly. Spread on wax paper lined cookie sheets. Let cool 1 hour. Break into bite-size pieces.

CHOCOLATE TRUFFLES

1. 3/4 Cup Butter
2. 3/4 Cup Cocoa
3. 1 Can (14 oz.) Sweetened Condensed Milk
4. 1 Tablespoon Vanilla Extract

In saucepan over low heat, melt butter, add cocoa and stir until smooth. Blend in sweetened condensed milk. Stir constantly until mixture is thick, smooth and glossy (about 4 minutes). Remove from heat and stir in vanilla. Chill 3 to 4 hours and shape into balls. Chill until firm, 1 to 2 hours. Store in refrigerator.

TOFFEE

1. 1 Cup Pecans (chopped)
2. 1/4 Cup Brown Sugar (packed)
3. 1/2 Cup Butter
4. 1/2 Cup Semi-Sweet Chocolate Chips

Grease square 9x9-inch pan. Spread pecans in pan. In saucepan, heat sugar and butter to boiling point, stirring constantly. Boil over medium heat, stirring constantly, for 7 minutes. Immediately spread mixture over nuts in pan. Sprinkle chocolate chips over hot mixture. Place baking sheet over pan so contained heat will melt chocolate chips. With knife, spread the melted chocolate over candy. While hot, cut into squares. Chill.

GLAZED PECANS

1. 1 Egg White
2. 3/4 Cup Brown Sugar
3. 1/2 Teaspoon Vanilla
4. 2 Cups Pecan Halves

Beat egg white until soft peak will stand. Gradually add sugar and vanilla. Fold in pecans. Place pecans on greased cookie sheet, about an inch apart. Bake at 400° for 30 minutes. Turn off oven and let stand in oven for another 30 minutes. Store in airtight container.

WHITE FUDGE

1. 3 Tablespoons Margarine
2. 3 Tablespoons Milk
3. 1 Package (15.4 oz.) Creamy White Frosting Mix
4. 1/2 Cup Chopped Nuts

Butter 9x5x3 inch loaf pan. In double boiler, melt margarine in milk and stir in dry frosting mix until smooth. Heat over rapidly boiling water for 5 minutes, stirring occasionally. Stir in nuts. Spread mixture in pan. Cool until firm and then cut into squares.

CHOCOLATE COCONUT DROPS

1. 2 Squares (1 oz. each) Unsweetened Chocolate
2. 1 Can (14 oz.) Sweetened Condensed Milk
3. 2 Cups Flaked Coconut
4. 1/2 Cup Chopped Walnuts

Preheat oven to 350°. In saucepan melt chocolate over low heat. Remove from heat and stir in milk, coconut and walnuts. Drop by teaspoonfuls onto ungreased cookie sheet. Place in oven and turn off heat. Leave about 15 minutes or until candy has glazed appearance. While warm, remove from cookie sheet.

CANDY TRIFLES

1. 1 Package (12 oz.) Semisweet Chocolate Chips
2. 1 Cup Spanish Peanuts
3. 2 Cups Chow Mein Noodles

In double boiler over hot water, melt chocolate pieces. Stir in nuts and noodles until well coated. Drop mixture by teaspoonfuls onto waxed paper. Chill until firm.

CARMALITAS

1. 1 Roll (18 oz.) Refrigerated Chocolate Chip Cookie Dough
2. 32 Vanilla Caramels
3. 1/4 Cup Light Cream or Evaporated Milk
4. 1 Cup Semi-Sweet Chocolate Chips

Slice cookie dough 1/4-inch thick and place on bottom of 9x9-inch pan. Pat to make even crust. Bake at 375° for 25 minutes. Cool slightly. Melt caramels and cream in double boiler. Sprinkle cookie dough with chocolate chips. Spread caramel mixture on top. Refrigerate 1-2 hours. Cut into squares. Makes 36 pieces.

PEANUT BUTTER FUDGE

1. 1 Package (10 oz.) Peanut Butter Chips
2. 1 Can (14 oz.) Sweetened Condensed Milk
3. 1/4 Cup Butter
4. 1 Package (6 oz.) Semi-Sweet Chocolate Chips

Melt peanut butter chips in large sauce pan. Add 1 cup sweetened condensed milk and 2 tablespoons butter. Stir. Remove from heat and spread mixture into wax paper lined 8-inch square pan. Melt chocolate chips with remaining milk and butter. Spread on top of peanut butter mixture. Chill 2 hours. Remove from refrigerator and slice.

BUTTERSCOTCH CANDY

1. 1 Package (12 oz.) Butterscotch Chips
2. 1 Package (6 oz.) Chocolate Chips
3. 2 1/2 Cups Chow Mein Noodles

Melt butterscotch and chocolate chips over double boiler. Add noodles and mix well. Drop by tablespoonfuls onto waxed paper. Cool until firm.

A lot of pies can be frozen, so making them ahead saves even more time.

MINI CHIPS CRESCENTS

1. 1 Can (8 oz.) Refrigerated Crescent Rolls
2. Ground Cinnamon
3. 1/2 Cup Semi-Sweet Mini-Chocolate Chips
4. Confectioner's Sugar

Unroll crescent rolls on ungreased cookie sheet to form
8 triangles. Lightly sprinkle cinnamon and
1 tablespoon mini chips on top of each triangle. Gently
press into dough. Starting at short side of triangle, roll
dough to opposite point. Bake at 375° for 10-12
minutes or until golden brown. Sprinkle sugar over top
and serve warm.

CHOCOLATE MARSHMALLOW MOUSSE

1. 1 Bar (7 oz.) Hershey's Milk Chocolate
2. 1 1/2 Cups Miniature Marshmallows
3. 1/3 Cup Milk
4. 1 Cup Chilled Whipping Cream

Break chocolate bar into pieces. In double boiler, melt
chocolate bar and marshmallows with milk. Cool to
room temperature. In small mixing bowl, beat
whipping cream until stiff. Fold into cooled chocolate
mixture and pour into dessert dishes. Cover and chill 1
to 2 hours until firm.

MOCHA MOUSSE

1. 2 Envelopes Whipped Topping Mix
2. 3 Cups Cold Milk
3. 1 Package Instant Chocolate Pudding Mix
4. 3 Tablespoons Coffee

In mixer bowl, beat whipped topping with 1 cup cold milk. Add remaining milk and pudding mix. Blend well and beat for 2 minutes. Blend in coffee and pour into dessert dishes.

CARAMEL POPCORN BALLS

1. 28 Caramels
2. 2 Tablespoons Water
3. 2 Quarts Salted Cooked Popcorn

Melt caramels and water in double boiler. Pour over cooked popcorn and toss until well coated. Shape into balls.

FUDGE PUDDING

1. 1 Package (3 1/2 oz.) Chocolate Pudding Mix
2. 2 Cups Milk
3. 1 Cup Semi-sweet Chocolate Chips

In saucepan combine pudding and milk. Cook over medium heat, stirring constantly, until mixture comes to a full boil. Remove from heat and stir in chocolate chips until they are melted. Spoon into dessert cups. Press plastic wrap directly onto surface and refrigerate until ready to serve.

STRAWBERRY TRIFLE

1. 2 Packages (3.4 oz. each) Instant Vanilla Pudding
2. 4 Cups Milk
3. 20 Vanilla Wafer Cookies
4. 2 Pints (12 oz.) Strawberries (hulled and sliced)

Combine pudding mix and milk and beat. Pour half of pudding into 2-quart bowl or trifle dish. Top with vanilla wafers, then sprinkle with strawberries. Top with remaining pudding. Cover and refrigerate at least 4 hours or up to 24 hours.

APPLE CRISP

1. 1/3 Cup Butter (softened)
2. 1 Cup Brown Sugar
3. 3/4 Cup Flour
4. 4 Cups Tart Apples (sliced)

Mix butter, sugar and flour. Place apple slices in 8x8-inch pan. Sprinkle butter topping over apples. Bake at 350° for 1 hour.

INDEX

APPETIZERS

Almond Delight Dip, 10
Artichoke Appetizer, 18
Artichoke Ranch Dip, 8
Bean and Cheese Dip, 8
Beer Bread, 19
Bleu Cheese Walnut Dip, 11
Bleu Vegetable Dip, 9
Caramel Fruit Dip, 11
Cheese Chili Appetizer, 15
Cocktail Sausage Balls, 13
Crab Appetizers, 18
Crab Delight, 15
Curry Dip, 9
Deviled Ham Log, 12
Dill Croutons, 17
Ham and Pimiento Spread, 19
Ham Crescent Snacks, 16
Mexican Avocado Dip, 8
Mini Quiches, 14
Monterey Cheese Crisps, 15
Nippy Shrimp, 16
Peppered Cheese Balls, 11
Potato Chip Cheese
   Appetizers, 12
Salami Rollups, 17
Salsa Cheese Dip, 9
7-up Biscuits, 20
Shrimp Dip, 10
Smoked Oyster Loaf, 12
Smokey Spread, 19
Spicy Pecans, 18
Tortellini Appetizers, 17
Tortilla Rollups, 14
Twist Sticks, 20
Veggie Dippin' Dip, 10
Wheat Cheese Snacks, 13
Yammy Biscuits, 21

BEEF

BBQ Flank Steak, 62
Bean Boats, 63
Beef and Cabbage Rolls, 56
Beef Brisket, 60
Beef Roast, 59
Cabbage and Beef Dish, 55
Chili Casserole, 63
Chili Meat Loaf, 53
Chili Stuffed Peppers, 64
Coke Roast, 60
Coney Island Burgers, 52
Easy Pot Roast, 61
Fiesta Dinner, 58
Flank Steak Supreme, 64
Frito Meat Balls, 53
Ground Beef and Pepper
   Skillet, 57
Hamburger Sloppy Joes, 58
Hot Meat Dish, 57
Meat and Potato Dinner, 56
Meat Pita Pockets, 52
Mexican Meatloaf, 53
Mustard Onion Chuck Roast, 59
Oven Pot Roast and Gravy, 61
Quick Meat Balls, 54
Ranch Style Spaghetti, 58
Sizzler Sirloin Steak, 62
Sour Cream Meatballs, 54
Spanish Hamburgers, 54
Spanish Stuffed Peppers, 55
Vegetable Meat Dish, 57
Zippy Beef Casserole, 52

BREADS

Beer Bread, 19
7-Up Biscuits, 20
Twist Sticks, 20
Yammy Biscuits, 21

CAKES

Angel Nut Cake/Frosting, 97
Apricot Cake, 101
Butter Cake, 98
Festive Cranberry Cake, 100
Lemon Cake/Frosting, 98
Rich Chocolate Cake, 99
Tomato Spice Cake, 99
Triple Fudge Cake, 101
Ugly Duckling Cake/
    Frosting, 100

CANDY

Butterscotch Candy, 110
Candy Trifles, 109
Carmalitas, 109
Chocolate Bites, 106
Chocolate Coconut Drops, 108
Chocolate Marshmallow
    Slices, 105
Chocolate Peanut Clusters, 105
Chocolate Truffles, 106
Glazed Pecans, 107
Peanut Butter Fudge, 110
Toffee, 107
White Fudge, 108

CHEESE

Bean and Cheese Dip, 8
Bleu Cheese Walnut Dip, 11
Bleu Vegetable Dip, 9
Cheese Chili Appetizer, 15
Monterey Cheese Crisps, 15
Peppered Cheese Ball, 11
Potato Chip Cheese
    Appetizers, 12
Salsa Cheese Dip, 9
Wheat Cheese Snacks, 13

CHICKEN (See Poultry)

COOKIES

Almond Bark Cookies, 101
Coconut Cookies, 102
Fudge Cookies, 103
Gold Brownies, 103
Lemon Cookies, 104
Lemon Whippersnaps, 102
Orange Coconut Balls, 102
Peanut Butter Candy
    Cookies, 103
Raisin Treats, 104

CORN

Corn Relish, 39
Corn Salad, 29
Scalloped Corn, 39

DESSERTS (see cakes, candy, cookies, pies, dessert, other)

DESSERTS, OTHER

Apple Crisp, 113
Caramel Popcorn Balls, 112
Chocolate Marshmallow
    Mousse, 111
Fudge Pudding, 112
Mini Chips Crescents, 111
Mocha Mousse, 112
Strawberry Trifle, 113

DIPS

Almond Delight Dip, 10
Artichoke Ranch Dip, 8
Bean and Cheese Dip, 8
Bleu Cheese Walnut Dip, 11
Bleu Vegetable Dip, 9
Caramel Fruit Dip, 11
Curry Dip, 9
Mexican Avocado Dip, 8
Salsa Cheese Dip, 9
Shrimp Dip, 10
Veggie Dippin' Dip, 10

FISH

Bacon Crisp Oysters, 87
Baked Orange Roughy, 82
Broccoli Tuna Casserole, 88
Buttermilk Fried Fillets, 82
Caesar's Fish, 84
Cordon Bleu Fish Fillets, 83
Easy Crab Dish, 86
Grilled Tuna Casserole, 88
Italian Scallops, 85
Lemon Dill Fish, 84
Marinated Grilled Shrimp, 86
Oyster Sausage Stew, 87
Pepper Shrimp, 85
Quick Tuna Casserole, 88
Quick Tuna Pot Pie, 89
Shrimp Marinara, 86
Spanish Fish, 83
Tater Tot Tuna, 89
Trout Almadine, 85

FROSTINGS

Angel Nut Frosting, 97
Lemon Cake Frosting, 98
Ugly Duckling Frosting, 100

HAM (SEE PORK)

PASTA

Fettucine Alfredo, 40
Pasta Salad, 33
Poppy Seed Noodles, 41
Seafood Pasta Salad, 33

PIES

Blueberry Pie, 92
Butter Pecan Pie, 94
Cookie Crust Ice Cream Pie, 94
German Chocolate Pie, 96
Key Lime Pie, 92
Koolaide Pie, 93
Malted Milk Pie, 97
Margarita Pie, 93
Peanut Butter Pie, 95
Pineapple-Lemon Pie, 92
Strawberry Pie, 95
Strawberry Mallow Pie, 95
Strawberry Yogurt Pie, 96
Vanilla Sour Cream Pie, 93

PORK

Franks and Crescents, 81
Grilled Pork Chops, 78
Ham in Madeira Wine, 79
Ham with Red-eye Gravy, 80
Honey Glazed Ham, 79
Hot Dog Tacos, 81
Mustard-Apricot Pork Chops, 78
Oven Braised Ham, 79
Oven Fried Pork Chops, 77
Pork Chop Casserole
    Supper, 77
Pork Chops with Red
    Cabbage, 75

Pork Stir-fry, 76
Roman Spaghetti, 80
Saucy Pork Chops, 76
Sausage Bake, 81
Spicy Chops, 75
Tex-Mex Chops, 78

POTATOES

Chicken Flavored Whipped
    Potatoes, 44
Country Style Potatoes, 44
Italian Potatoes, 43
Marshmallow Topped Sweet
    Potatoes, 46
New Potato Vinaigrette, 45
Parsley New Potatoes, 42
Potatoes Au Gratin, 44
Quick Potato Cheese Bake, 43
Scalloped Potatoes, 43
Stuffed Baked Sweet
    Potatoes, 45

POULTRY

Baked Chicken and Beans, 72
Broccoli Chicken, 65
Cherry Sherry Chicken, 66
Chicken Meatballs, 74
Chicken Noodle Casserole, 73
Chicken Risotto, 66
Chicken Spinach Bake, 68
Chicken Wild Rice
    Casserole, 67
Club Chicken, 65
Confetti Chicken, 71
Fiesta Chicken, 70
Hawaiian Chicken, 73
Herb Lemon Chicken, 69
Honey Mustard Chicken, 68

Italian Chicken, 69
Nutty Chicken, 67
Onion Ring Chicken, 71
Pecan Chicken, 71
Potato Mustard Chicken, 70
Swiss Chicken Casserole, 67
Tangy Chicken, 72
Turkey Rollups, 74
Zesty Crisp Chicken, 69

RICE

Cumin Rice, 47
Dirty Rice, 47
French Onion Rice, 46
Onions and Herb Rice, 46
Rice Salad, 32

SALADS

Avocado Grapefruit Salad, 28
Carrot Salad, 31
Cold Slaw, 28
Corn Salad, 29
Cucumber Salad, 29
Frozen Cranberry Salad, 25
Frozen Pineapple Cranberry
    Salad, 27
Fruit Cocktail Salad, 24
Green Bean Salad, 31
Ice Cream Salad, 24
Layered Fruit Salad, 26
Lime Coke Salad, 24
Mandarin Salad/Orange
    Juice Dressing, 27
Mango Salad, 25
Marinated Asparagus Salad, 29
Nutty Banana Salad, 28
Orange Salad, 25
Pasta Salad, 33

Pea Salad, 30
Rice Salad, 32
Seafood Salad, 32
Seafood Pasta Salad, 33
Shrimp and Rice Salad, 32
Sliced Frozen Fruit Salad, 26
Spinach Salad, 30
Sunny Spinach Salad, 30
Super Spinach Salad, 31
Waldorf Salad, 26

SQUASH

Baked Squash Casserole, 48
Potato Chip Squash
    Casserole, 48
Squash Dressing, 48
Stir Fried Zucchini, 46
Zucchini and Walnuts, 49

VEGETABLES
Asparagus in Lemon Butter, 36
Asparagus with Curry Sauce, 37
Baked Squash Casserole, 48
Brussels Sprouts, 38
Cheesy Cauliflower, 39
Chicken Flavored Whipped
    Potatoes, 44
Corn Relish, 39
Country Style Potatoes, 44
Cumin Rice, 47
Dill Carrots, 38
Dirty Rice, 47
Fettucine Alfredo, 40
French Onion Rice, 46
Fried Green Tomatoes, 49
Green Been Casserole, 40
Green Chili Cassrole, 40
Italian Potatoes, 43
Italian Style Broccoli, 37
Lemon Asparagus and Bak
    Carrots, 36

Marinated Artichoke Hearts, 36
Marshmallow Topped Sweet
    Potatoes, 46
Marvelous Mushrooms, 41
New Potato Vinaigrette, 45
Okra Succotash, 42
Onions and Herb Rice, 46
Parsley New Potatoes, 42
Poppy Seed Noodles, 41
Potato Chip Squash
    Casserole, 48
Potatoes Au Gratin, 44
Quick Potato Cheese Bake, 43
Sauteed Broccoli, 37
Sauteed Spinach, 47
Scalloped Corn, 39
Scalloped Potatoes, 43
Spicy Potatoes, 42
Squash Dressing, 48
Stir Fried Mushrooms With
    Bacon, 41
Stir Fry Zucchini, 46
Stuffed Baked Sweet
    Potatoes, 45
Zucchini and Walnuts, 49

For Additional Copies...

Please send me...

_____ copies of *The Four Ingredient Cookbooks* @ $19.95 each	$_____
_____ copies of *The Diabetic Four Ingredient Cookbook* @ $19.95 each	$_____
Postage & handling @ $3.50 each	$_____
Sub-Total	$_____
Texas residents add 8.25% sales tax per book @ $1.93 each	$_____
Canadian orders add additional $6.60 per book	$_____
Total Enclosed	$_____

❏ Check enclosed made payable to "Coffee and Cale"

Or charge to my

❏ VISA   ❏ MasterCard   ❏ Discover   *(Canada - credit card only)*

Card # _____   Exp. Date _____

Ship to:

Name_____

Address _____Apt.# _____

City _____ State _____ Zip _____

E-mail address _____

Phone _____

(Must have for Credit Card Orders)

Coffee & Cale

P.O. Box 2121 • Kerrville, TX 78029 • 1-800-757-0838

www.fouringredientcookbook.com • email:areglen@ktc.com

For Wholesale Information: • (830) 895-5528

Also Available

Our *original* soft cover cookbooks!

___ copies of *The Four Ingredient Cookbook* @ $12.90 each $_____

___ copies of *More of the Four Ingredient Cookbook* @ $12.90 each $_____

___ copies of *Low-Fat & Light Four Ingredient Cookbook* @ $12.90 each $_____

Special Savings!!!

Buy any 3 original soft cover cookbooks for only $23.50!!! $_____

above prices include shipping & handling of $2.95 per book

Texas residents add 8.25% sales tax $_____

Canadian orders add additional $3.30 per book $_____

Total Enclosed $_____

❏ Check enclosed made payable to "Coffee and Cale"

Or charge to my

❏ VISA   ❏ MasterCard   ❏ Discover   *(Canada - credit card only)*

Card #_____ Exp. Date_____

Ship to:

Name _____

Address_____Apt.# _____

City _____ State _____ Zip_____

E-mail address _____

Phone_____

(Must have for Credit Card Orders)

Coffee & Cale
P.O. Box 2121 • Kerrville, TX 78029 • 1-800-757-0838
www.fouringredientcookbook.com • email:areglen@ktc.com
For Wholesale Information: • (830) 895-5528

For Additional Copies...

Please send me...

_____ copies of *The Four Ingredient Cookbooks* @ $19.95 each $_____

_____ copies of *The Diabetic Four Ingredient Cookbook* @ $19.95 each $_____

Postage & handling @ $3.50 each $_____

Sub-Total $_____

Texas residents add 8.25% sales tax per book @ $1.93 each $_____

Canadian orders add additional $6.60 per book $_____

Total Enclosed $_____

❏ Check enclosed made payable to "Coffee and Cale"

Or charge to my

❏ VISA   ❏ MasterCard   ❏ Discover   *(Canada - credit card only)*

Card # _____ Exp. Date _____

Ship to:

Name_____

Address _____Apt.# _____

City _____ State _____ Zip _____

E-mail address _____

Phone _____
(Must have for Credit Card Orders)

Coffee & Cale
P.O. Box 2121 • Kerrville, TX 78029 • 1-800-757-0838
www.fouringredientcookbook.com • email:areglen@ktc.com
For Wholesale Information: • (830) 895-5528

Also Available

Our *original* soft cover cookbooks!

___ copies of *The Four Ingredient Cookbook* @ $12.90 each $_____

___ copies of *More of the Four Ingredient Cookbook* @ $12.90 each $_____

___ copies of *Low-Fat & Light Four Ingredient Cookbook* @ $12.90 each $_____

Special Savings!!!

Buy any 3 original soft cover cookbooks for only $23.50!!! $_____

above prices include shipping & handling of $2.95 per book

Texas residents add 8.25% sales tax $_____

Canadian orders add additional $3.30 per book $_____

Total Enclosed $_____

❏ Check enclosed made payable to "Coffee and Cale"

Or charge to my

❏ VISA   ❏ MasterCard   ❏ Discover   *(Canada - credit card only)*

Card #_____ Exp. Date_____

Ship to:

Name _____

Address_____Apt.# _____

City _____ State _____ Zip_____

E-mail address _____

Phone_____

(Must have for Credit Card Orders)

Coffee & Cale

P.O. Box 2121 • Kerrville, TX 78029 • 1-800-757-0838

www.fouringredientcookbook.com • email:areglen@ktc.com

For Wholesale Information: • (830) 895-5528